SOUTH CAROLINA
Hometown Cookbook

Table Rock State Park in Spring

Table Rock State Park in Autumn

SOUTH CAROLINA
Hometown Cookbook

by Sheila Simmons and Kent Whitaker

Great American Publishers
www.GreatAmericanPublishers.com
TOLL-FREE 1.888.854.5954

Great American Publishers

171 Lone Pine Church Road • Lena, MS 39094

TOLL-FREE 1.888.854.5954 • www.GreatAmericanPublishers.com

ISBN 978-1-934817-10-0

10 9 8 7 6 5 4 3 2

by Sheila Simmons & Kent Whitaker

Designed by Roger & Sheila Simmons

South Carolina

Contents

Introduction

This STATE HOMETOWN COOKBOOK SERIES has been a blessing from God. When my husband, Roger, and I took the big leap of faith to start our own publishing company, we knew that a state cookbook series was in our future. By this time, Kent and I had known each other for years and I've always had a great amount of respect for his cooking and recipe-building skills. So he was a natural first choice for the series.

Originally, I wanted to set him up with a different co-author. God's plan is always best, and this time He had a different plan than mine. So, in the end, it was Kent and me doing the series and beginning with the *Tennessee Hometown Cookbook* in 2006, we've never looked back.

South Carolina is our sixth state in the series and it seems that each one is better than the last. I fall in love with every state we add to the series and South Carolina is no exception. From the beautiful palmetto trees lining the coast of the Low Country to the Up Country's majestic mountains plus the sand hills, lowlands, and crystal clear lakes in between... there is something for everyone to love in the Palmetto State.

Quite simply, South Carolina is home to great food. From ***Beef Spare Ribs with BBQ Sauce*** to ***Coastal Carolina Lowcountry Red Rice*** to Charleston's world-famous ***82 Queen's She-Crab Soup***, everywhere you turn, you are met with southern hospitality and delicious southern cooking.

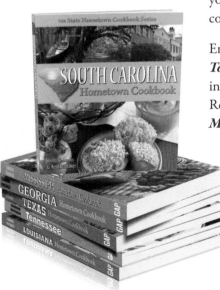

Enjoy South Carolina's abundant fresh produce in recipes like ***Okra with Tomatoes***—a recipe originally featured in *The Beaufort Cookbook* published in 1965 and shared with us by the South Carolina Department of Parks, Recreation and Tourism. Or cook the sumptuous local seafood in ***Fish Muddle***. Or ***Adluh's Carolina Breaded Shrimp*** featuring Adluh Flour, a South Carolina business.

From ***Carolina Country Applesauce Spice Cake*** to ***Lady Baltimore Cake with South Carolina Peaches***, ***Charleston Huguenot Torte*** to ***Butterscotch Peach Crisp***, ***Easy Plantation Cookies*** to ***Rena's Sugared Pecans***... a little something sweet from South Carolina is like heaven on your plate.

One of the best ways to fall in love with the beauty of South Carolina is by visiting the many fun festivals held across the state each year. Throughout this book, you will enjoy fun stories and pictures about many food-related festivals across the Palmetto State. From the **South Carolina Apple Festival** in Westminster, to Little River's **World Famous Blue Crab Festival,** the **Beaufort Shrimp Festival** to Gaffney's **South Carolina Peach Festival,** and so many more, there's a celebration for everyone to adore.

My gratitude and Kent's goes to the many wonderful people associated with these festivals who were infinitely helpful and generous with their time. Thank you for helping make this book better. Our sincerest appreciation also goes to Pam Edwards, Tori Kelly, and Pat Ashton for their tireless research, to Brooke Craig for keeping the place running while we write and research, to Cyndi Clark for making our work pretty, to Diane Adams for her effortless office management, and to Christy Campbell and the best sales team around: Krista Griffin, Anita Musgrove, Christy Kent Campbell, Nichole Stewart, Melissa Coleman, and Gena Scott, thank you all for giving our work purpose and adding spice to our days. As always, a big THANK YOU goes to our families for their unwavering support; Ally and Macee, Roger, Ryan, Nicholas and Granny—you are at the heart of all we do.

"Dum Spiro, Spero. While I breath, I hope." This is South Carolina's state motto. Our greatest hope for this latest edition in the STATE HOMETOWN COOKBOOK SERIES is that you enjoy reading it and cooking from it as much as we enjoyed writing it. Thank you for sharing in this taste of South Carolina's southern hospitality.

Wishing you many happy kitchen memories,

Sheila Simmons & Kent Whitaker

"With man, this is impossible, but not with God.
All things are possible with God."
Mark 10:27 (NIV)

Appetizers

Mayo Tater Wedges, page 15

Palmetto Cheese
The Pimento Cheese with Soul!

While Palmetto Cheese—The Pimento Cheese with Soul—was born in the Lowcountry of South Carolina, it originated with Sassy Henry whipping up batches of her pimento cheese recipe while living in Atlanta and tailgating at Braves games.

In 2002, Sassy, her husband Brian, and their two children moved to Pawleys Island, to run the historic Sea View Inn. It is there that Palmetto Cheese was featured as an appetizer each week during the summer Lowcountry shrimp boils. It quickly became a favorite of guests and locals who urged the Henrys to introduce the public to their authentic southern pimento cheese recipe.

In 2006, the couple introduced Palmetto Cheese to the Southeast market. The hope was that by using the highest quality ingredients, customers would connect with childhood memories of pimento cheese and feel the same passion for the product they had growing up.

In 2003, using Sassy Henry's recipe, Vertrella Brown, a Pawleys Island native and cook at Sea View Inn for over 25 years specializing in Gullah and Lowcountry cuisine, began producing batches of Palmetto Cheese for delighted guests. Her image personifies the soulful flavor embodied in this unique, southern recipe. This is why she is featured on the lid and we refer to it as "The Pimento Cheese with Soul".

Palmetto Cheese is great to serve as a dip with vegetables, on a cracker, sandwich, burger or eggs and in your favorite baked recipes. It is available at over 5,000 locations in 31 states and growing. Fans will tell you that Palmetto Cheese is the most authentic southern recipe on the market. And, in 2014, Palmetto Cheese became the top selling pimento cheese on grocery shelves today.

Pawleys Island
Specialty Foods

P.O. Box 1481 • Pawleys Island, SC 29585
1-888-406-9823
www.pimentocheese.com
www.facebook.com/palmettocheese

Personally Fit
Peach Morning Smoothie

3 South Carolina peaches, peeled, pitted and sliced
1 medium banana, halved
1½ cups skim milk
1 cup lemon or vanilla fat-free yogurt
2 tablespoons honey
1 individual-serving packet cinnamon spice instant oatmeal

Purée all ingredients in a blender until smooth. Blend with ice, if preferred. Serve in chilled glasses.

Matt Fulmer, Columbia
South Carolina Peach Council

Peach Sangria

4 (750-milliliter) bottles red wine
1¼ cups sugar (or sugar substitute equivalent)
4 fresh South Carolina peaches, peeled, pitted and sliced
2 Granny Smith apples, peeled, cored and sliced
2 bananas, peeled and sliced
2 cinnamon sticks, crushed
3 liters lemon-lime flavored (regular or diet) soda

In a large pitcher, combine red wine, sugar, peaches, apples, bananas and crushed cinnamon sticks. Refrigerate 6 hours or overnight. When ready to serve, stir in lemon-lime soda.

South Carolina Peach Council

Watermelon Slushie

4 cups cubed seedless
   watermelon
10 ice cubes

⅓ cup fresh lime juice
¼ cup sugar
⅛ teaspoon salt

Place watermelon and ice into a blender. Pour in lime juice, sugar and salt. Blend until smooth.

Pageland Watermelon Festival
Pageland • 3rd Full Weekend in July

Come and enjoy live music and entertainment as you walk through the streets of downtown Pageland. See one of the largest parades on Saturday morning that will provide plenty of entertainment by itself. Savor the delicious variety of foods and the beautiful wares of the crafters. Children will enjoy a variety of events throughout the day. Don't forget the old-fashion seed spittin' and watermelon eatin' contests for all ages. Enjoy reminiscing about yesteryear with our classic car show and admire the talents displayed at the festival rodeo. Then enjoy the company of friends and visitors at the end of each day, and take in the music and entertainment of live bands.

843.672.6400 • www.pagelandchamber.com

Leslie's Bloody Mary Appetizer

Grape tomatoes
Vodka
Old Bay seasoning

So good you'll take back stuff you never stole!!

Wash tomatoes and put in a serving bowl. Pour vodka into a martini glass to ½ full. Fill another martini glass ½ full with Old Bay seasoning. Guests will dip tomatoes in vodka then seasoning and eat. I PROMISE! It tastes just like a Bloody Mary!

Leslie Haywood, Charleston
Inventor and founder of Grill Charms • www.grillcharms.com

Leslie Haywood

South Carolina Boiled Peanuts

6 quarts water (purified or spring, if possible)
1½ cups kosher salt (not table salt)*
4 pounds raw green peanuts

In a big stockpot, bring water to a boil adding salt as it begins to boil. When salt is dissolved, add peanuts gently (so you don't splash hot water on yourself). Boil peanuts at least 5 hours; it can take up to 6 or 7 hours. Add water as needed, but don't add any more salt. After 5 hours, check for doneness every 20 minutes or so. When done, the peanuts will be soft yet still firm. If they cook too long they may become mushy. Under-cooked a tad bit is better than over-cooked every time.

*Note: Table salt has a different taste than kosher salt and can turn your peanuts black, dark or cause them to be too salty.

Darnel Brantley, Clemson

I learned how to boil peanuts growing up in Clemson. You may not think it's hard, but there is a trick to boiling peanuts. This recipe will help you perfect your peanut-boiling skills. Once you get this down-home salted version down, you can add other seasonings such as Cajun seasoning, garlic powder, hot sauce or whatever you feel like trying. But to me, the plain old salted version is best.

South Carolina Pelion Peanut Party
Pelion • 2nd Weekend in August

"Peanuts for the Good Life!" Celebrating the South Carolina Official State Snack, the boiled peanut, our progressive, yet rural, agricultural community provides a safe and family-friendly venue for your enjoyment of our boiled peanuts! Join us for 2 days of yummy festival food, crafts, car show, softball contest, talent show, exhibits, parade, Princess Pageant, cooking contest, amusement rides, and country/rock and roll entertainment.

803.606.9522 or 803.785.3272
www.scpeanutparty.com

Toasted Pumpkin Seeds

Wash pumpkin seeds to remove strings; pat dry with paper towels. Spread seeds in a single layer on cookie sheet. Let stand 2 to 3 days, stirring occasionally to prevent mold. To toast, spread seeds on a jelly-roll pan. Bake in a 350° oven for 15 minutes or until lightly browned, stirring occasionally. Or, toast seeds in a small skillet over low heat, in a little hot butter or margarine, cooking until browned, stirring occasionally. Toss with dried fruits and serve.

South Carolina Department of Agriculture

Mayo Tater Wedges

4 large baking potatoes
½ cup mayonnaise
½ tablespoon hot sauce
½ tablespoon Italian seasoning
Salt and pepper
Cornmeal or cornbread mix

My mom gave me this recipe. She used it often with homemade wedges and sometimes on steak fries from the freezer section at the store. Both were very good, but I prefer the home-cut wedges.

Preheat oven to 375°. Wash potatoes and cut each into 6 thick wedges. (Or use thawed frozen steak fries.) Combine mayonnaise, hot sauce, Italian seasoning, salt and pepper. Coat potato wedges evenly with mayo mixture, and then dredge in cornmeal. Arrange on a greased baking sheet and bake 45 minutes or until potatoes are tender.

Lauren Caldwell, University of South Carolina

Easy Stuffed Mushrooms

12 large mushrooms
2 tablespoons chopped onion
2 tablespoons butter
½ cup chopped pecans
½ cup breadcrumbs
1 teaspoon lemon juice
½ teaspoon salt

This recipe is perfect for oven or grill.

Wash mushrooms. Remove and chop stems. Sauté onion in butter until soft. Add chopped stems, pecans, breadcrumbs, lemon juice and salt. Mix well and cook until heated through. Mound mushroom caps with stuffing. Broil 4 minutes.

Stephanie Frey/istock/thinkstock

Gamecock Tailgate Stuffed Peppers

1 (16-ounce) tube ground sausage
30 jalapeño peppers
1 (8-ounce) package cream cheese,
   softened
1 (8-ounce) bag shredded taco cheese
Worcestershire sauce or steak sauce to
   taste (optional)
Real bacon bits

Brown sausage; drain and cool. Slice peppers in half lengthwise. Remove seeds and rinse. (If you have time, you can soak peppers in milk.) In a large bowl, combine sausage, cream cheese and shredded cheese. If desired, add a few drops of Worcestershire sauce or even a dash of steak sauce. Add in Real bacon bits to taste; mix. Spoon filling into each pepper half. Grill 8 to 10 minutes (or bake at 350°) until cheese is melted and puffy with a hint of gold color.

Mike Hicks, Go Gamecocks, Columbia

Classic Stuffed Deviled Eggs

15 large eggs
3 tablespoons mayonnaise
1 tablespoon sugar
1 tablespoon Dijon mustard
1 tablespoon cider vinegar
1 teaspoon hot sauce
1 teaspoon Worcestershire sauce
⅛ teaspoon salt
Paprika
Fresh herb sprigs for garnish

Place eggs in large saucepan. Add enough water to measure at least 1 inch above eggs. Cover and quickly bring to a boil. Remove from heat and let stand, covered, in hot water 20 minutes. Carefully drain hot water and immediately run cold water over eggs or place them in ice water until they have completely cooled. Shell eggs. Slice in half lengthwise and remove yolks into a bowl. Combine yolks with remaining ingredients, except garnish, and mix well until creamy. Place yolk mixture into zip-close bag. Cut off one corner of bag and pipe stuffing into egg whites. Garnish with fresh herb sprigs.

Meg Tarbox, Georgetown

Christine's Goat Cheese Stuffed Figs

This is one of my favorite summer dishes. I prefer Brown Turkey figs, and I try to use the freshest possible. Fresh South Carolina goat cheese from local farms can be found at farmer's markets. Grilling makes the sugars in the fig caramelize and the goat cheese melt slightly.

12 fresh Brown Turkey figs
1 (4-ounce) package goat/chèvre cheese
½ pound prosciutto, thinly sliced

Split each fig lengthwise. Scoop out a grape-sized ball of goat cheese; place in fig's center. Close fig back together. Wrap fig in a slice of prosciutto and secure with a bamboo skewer or toothpick. Repeat until all figs are used. Grill the figs, over indirect flame, a few minutes until cheese melts slightly.

Christine Harmel, Charleston

Dawn's Stuffed Pickled Jalapeños

1 (15-ounce) jar whole pickled jalapeños
Cream cheese, softened, to taste
Shredded sharp Cheddar cheese to taste
Spoonful mayonnaise
Salt and pepper to taste

Adjust this recipe to your own taste. I prefer the pickled whole jalapeños that come in a jar rather than fresh jalapeños.

Cut jalapeños in half lengthwise and remove seeds. Combine remaining ingredients and stuff peppers. Serve cold or heat slightly in oven or microwave.

Dawn Gleuck Britt, Columbia

Leslie Haywood

Easy Artichoke Appetizer Dip

I make this easy appetizer all of the time. Serve hot with pita chips. It's quick and tasty!

1 (14-ounce) can artichoke hearts, chopped
1 cup mayonnaise
1 cup grated fresh Parmesan cheese

Mix all ingredients. Bake in small baking dish at 350° for 30 minutes. Serve with pita chips.

Leslie Haywood, Charleston
Inventor and founder of Grill Charms • www.grillcharms.com

Seafood Cheese Ball

1 (8-ounce) package cream cheese, softened
1 teaspoon horseradish
1 to 2 drops Worcestershire sauce

1 (6-ounce) can crabmeat, flaked
1 tablespoon lemon juice
2 to 3 tablespoons seafood seasoning
1 cup chopped pecans (optional)

Mix cream cheese, horseradish, Worcestershire sauce, crabmeat, lemon juice and seafood seasoning together; form into a ball. Cover and chill 2 hours or longer, until firm. (Can be made a day ahead.) Before serving, roll in pecans to coat, if desired. Serve chilled with crackers.

Jalapeño Palmetto Cheese Fritters

1½ cups all-purpose flour
1½ cups buttermilk
2½ cups panko breadcrumbs
1 (12-ounce) carton Palmetto Cheese with Jalapeños (Original or Bacon can also be substituted)
3 cups oil for frying
Red pepper relish, optional

Place flour, buttermilk and breadcrumbs each in a separate bowl to create a breading station. (You may need more or less of these ingredients.) Form 1 tablespoon Palmetto Cheese into a ball. Roll in flour, then buttermilk, then breadcrumbs. If you can still see cheese, roll in buttermilk and breadcrumbs one more time (no additional flour is needed). Place on a sheet pan or plate. Once all the balls are rolled, freezer for 30 minutes. This will firm everything up and make the fritters easier to fry. In a small saucepan, heat oil to 350°. Slowly add fritters to oil and fry until golden. Remove with a slotted spoon and place on paper towels to drain. Serve with pepper relish or your favorite dipping sauce. Enjoy!

Palmetto Cheese • Pawleys Island Specialty Foods
www.pimentocheese.com

Yemassee Shrimp Festival

Yemassee • 3rd Weekend in September

For 18 years, the people of Yemassee, a small community of about 800, have opened their arms to all of the Lowcountry for an annual Shrimp Festival to celebrate everything shrimp. With the Lighted Boat Parade, a mud run, a fireworks display and more, this fun family festival is sure to impress. After all, there is "Nothin' Finer than the Shrimp in Carolina."

843.589.2120 • www.yemasseeshrimpfestival.com

Coastal Shrimp Fritters

**1 pound shrimp, cooked, peeled and
   deveined
1 cup all-purpose flour
1 teaspoon baking powder
1 teaspoon salt
1 teaspoon pepper
2 large eggs
¼ cup beer
1 medium onion, chopped
1 jalapeño pepper, minced
2 teaspoons minced garlic
½ to 1 teaspoon seafood seasoning**

Chop shrimp and set aside. In a bowl, beat flour, baking powder, salt, pepper, eggs and beer with an electric mixer on medium speed until smooth. Stir in shrimp, onion, pepper, garlic and seafood seasoning. Cover and chill 2 hours. Fry in hot oil in small batches using tablespoon-size portions. Cook until golden brown; drain on a paper towel. While hot, sprinkle with additional seasonings, if desired.

Charleston Crab Rangoon

1 (6-ounce) can white crabmeat, drained, flaked or fresh
4 ounces cream cheese, softened
2 green onions, thinly sliced
¼ cup mayonnaise
12 wonton wrappers

Preheat oven to 350°. In a large bowl, combine crabmeat, cream cheese, onions and mayonnaise. Spray a muffin tin with nonstick spray. Place 1 wonton wrapper in each of 12 muffin cups. Fill each with equal amounts crab mixture. Fold wrapper edges over crab mixture and pinch together. Bake 15 to 20 minutes until edges are golden brown and filling is hot. Allow to rest and cool for a few minutes before serving.

Hilton Head Island Oyster Festival
Hilton Head • 2nd Weekend in November

Steamed, fried, raw, grilled and more... there are many ways to eat oyster at the Hilton Head Island Oyster Festival. Join us for a full day of live music and so many more activities for the whole family. All proceeds benefit the Hilton Head Island Recreation Association's Children's Scholarship Fund.

843.681.7273 • www.islandreccenter.org

South Carolina Crab Dip

1 (0.46-ounce) packet vegetable
    dip seasoning mix
1 (16-ounce) container sour cream
1 cup crumbled cooked crabmeat

Mix all ingredients in a bowl and cover. Refrigerate at least 1 hour before serving.

Kassandra

Tomato Pie Dip

1 (28-ounce) can diced tomatoes, drained
    (or 3 to 4 fresh tomatoes, diced)
1 tablespoon cornstarch
¼ cup cooked and chopped bacon
1 teaspoon each salt and pepper, divided
1 (15-ounce) carton ricotta cheese
1 (12-ounce) carton Palmetto Cheese
    (Original, Jalapeño, or Bacon)
1 tablespoon chopped fresh basil

Preheat oven to 375°. Combine tomatoes, cornstarch, bacon and ½ teaspoon each salt and pepper. Pour into a 9x9-inch casserole dish. In a mixing bowl, combine ricotta, Palmetto Cheese and basil; season with ½ teaspoon each salt and pepper. Spread over tomato mixture and bake 30 minutes. Serve with pita chips or the dipping chip of your choice.

Palmetto Cheese • Pawleys Island Specialty Foods
www.pimentocheese.com

Toasted Italian Shrimp Crisps

1 (11-ounce) can refrigerated thin
    pizza crust
¼ cup Zesty Italian dressing
2 teaspoons Italian seasoning

½ cup sliced olives
½ cup salad shrimp
⅓ cup grated Parmesan cheese

Preheat oven 350°. Place unrolled crust on a treated baking sheet; press into 12x15-inch rectangle. Bake about 5 minutes until firm. Brush with dressing; top with remaining ingredients. Return to the oven and bake an additional 10 minutes or until crust is golden brown. Cut into appetizer-sized squares.

Chanel's Tasty Fruit Salsa

2 ripe mangoes, diced and peeled*
1 to 2 tablespoons chopped fresh cilantro
1 to 2 peppers (your choice), chopped
2 green onions, chopped
Juice of 1 lime
½ to 1 teaspoon agave nectar or honey
    (optional)
Salt to taste

If you don't have mangoes, use pineapple, peaches, strawberries or any combination. You can have a new experience every time you make this versatile recipe by trying different combinations of fruit and peppers. I like to make it with jalapeño or serrano peppers. If you don't like the heat, use bell pepper. Anyway you make it, this is great with chips or served over grilled chicken, fish or pork.

Mix first 5 ingredients. Depending on how sweet your mangoes are, add agave nectar or honey to taste. Add salt to taste.

Note: Mangoes have a very large seed, so they cannot be sliced through the center. It's easier to slice off the sides and dice the pulp before peeling, then scoop the diced pulp from the skin.

Chanel Jack, Charleston
The Navy Wives of South Carolina Recipes

Bread & Breakfast

Peach Morning Muffins, page 32

Geechee Fried Corn Cakes

½ cup chopped onion
½ cup diced bell pepper
1 to 2 tablespoons butter
1 tablespoon chopped celery
¾ cup self-rising flour
¾ cup self-rising cornmeal
⅔ cup buttermilk
1 beaten egg

1 cup fresh or frozen corn, cooked
   and drained
3 tablespoons sugar
1 teaspoon garlic salt
1 teaspoon black pepper
1 teaspoon ground red pepper
Dash hot sauce
Oil for frying

Sauté onion and bell pepper in a small skillet with butter. Combine in a bowl with remaining ingredients, except oil, and mix well. Set aside for a few minutes to allow flour and cornmeal to activate. Drop by spoonfuls into hot oil in a cast iron skillet. Brown on one side; flip and brown until golden on the other side. Drain on paper towels.

Janet's Broccoli Cornbread

1 (10-ounce) package frozen
   broccoli, thawed and drained
1 medium onion, chopped
6 ounces cottage cheese
6 ounces sour cream

1 stick (½ cup) butter, melted
4 eggs, beaten
1 (8.5-ounce) box Jiffy Corn Muffin
   Mix

Preheat oven to 400°. Combine broccoli, onion, cottage cheese, sour cream, butter and eggs; mix well. Add corn muffin mix and continue mixing. Spray 8x8-inch pan with nonstick spray. Add batter to pan and bake 40 minutes or until brown on top and tester inserted comes out clean.

Janet Swope Wade, Aiken

South Carolina Cornbread Festival
Columbia • 1st Weekend in April

The North Columbia Business Association, in partnership with the City of Columbia, Richland County, and Pepsi-Cola bring you the South Carolina Cornbread Festival and 5K Run/Walk. The event takes place at the corner of the 2800 block of Main Street and Newman Street, in North Columbia. This popular festival offers fun and excitement for the whole family with a 5K Run/Walk, Cornbread Cook-Off, Children's Cook-Off, Little Miss Muffin Pageant, live music, and more.

803.840.5270 • www.sccornbreadfestival.com

Cast Iron Skillet Cornbread

2 cups yellow cornmeal
1 cup all-purpose flour
4 teaspoons baking powder
¾ teaspoon salt
1 teaspoon sugar
1 large egg, beaten
1½ cups buttermilk
2 to 3 tablespoons bacon grease or
    shortening

Preheat oven to 425°. In a large bowl, combine cornmeal, flour, baking powder, salt and sugar. Add egg and buttermilk; mix well. Heat bacon grease in a 9-inch cast iron skillet over medium heat. Pour in batter and cook 2 to 3 minutes, without stirring, until edges are slightly brown or golden. Place skillet in oven and bake 30 minutes, or until golden brown. Cool slightly before slicing to serve.

Bill White, Clemson

Ham and Pepper Cornbread

4 eggs, beaten
1 cup flour
1 cup yellow cornmeal
½ cup chopped ham or Real bacon bits
1 tablespoon baking powder
1 teaspoon salt
¾ cup milk
1 tablespoon vegetable oil
1½ tablespoons chopped jalapeño pepper
1 (11-ounce) can whole-kernel corn, drained

This combines pork and jalapeño peppers. My grandfather used to joke about it all of the time. He was from Charleston and said he used to eat cracklin' cornbread, but his dentist made him stop because he broke too many teeth! So my grandmother started using soft ham or sausage.

Preheat oven to 375°. Combine eggs, flour, cornmeal, ham, baking powder, salt, milk and vegetable oil. Add jalapeño and corn. Do not overmix but make sure all dry ingredients are moistened. Pour into greased muffin pan. Bake 25 minutes or until golden brown. Serve hot.

Miss B., Beaufort

Drayton Hall, Charleston

Bill Stamatis/istock/thinkstock

Heather's Simple White Bread

¼ cup sugar
2 cups warm water (110°)
1½ tablespoons active dry yeast
¼ cup vegetable oil plus extra for bread pan and bowl
1½ teaspoons salt
6 cups bread flour, divided

In large mixing bowl, dissolve sugar in warm water. Do not make the water too hot, or it will kill the yeast. Add yeast to sugar water. When it begins to look creamy, stir in oil, salt and 5 cups flour. Dough will be heavy and difficult to stir by hand. Spread remaining flour on work area and place dough on floured surface. Oil bowl and set aside.

Flour hands well and knead dough, placing heel of dominant hand into center of dough and push away from your body, toward the work surface. Grab edge of dough and fold it back on itself. Turn dough and repeat, kneading 10 minutes. Roll dough into a ball and place into oiled bowl. Turn several times to coat. Cover with damp cloth and place in warm, non-drafty area. Allow to rise 1 hour or until doubled in size.

When double in size, punch dough down, being careful not to punch too hard, which breaks down all air pockets, creating a dense loaf. Divide dough in half and press into roughly two 12x6-inch rectangles. Shape dough by rolling it into log shape. Tuck ends under and place in oiled 9x5-inch loaf pans. Allow to rise until slightly above rim.

While dough is rising, preheat oven to 350°. Bake approximately 30 minutes. Firmly tap top of loaf, when done it will have a hollow sound. Place on a wire rack and cool 5 minutes. Remove from pans and cool completely on wire rack.

Heather Solos, Moncks Corner

Adluh's Buttermilk Cheese Muffin Tin Biscuits

1 pound (3 cups) Adluh Yellow Flake Biscuit Mix
½ cup shredded sharp Cheddar cheese
1½ cups buttermilk

Pour Adluh Biscuit Mix into a bowl, and add cheese. Add buttermilk and mix. Scoop equal portions into greased muffin tins, bake at 400° for 25 minutes or until golden brown. I suggest you brush tops with butter. This recipe makes about 12 to 13 biscuits.

Variation: Increase cheese to 1 cup and add 1 teaspoon each garlic powder and oregano for delicious Adluh's Garlic Cheese Muffin Tin Biscuits.

Frank Workman, Columbia
Adluh Flour (www.adluh.com)

Adluh Flour Mills, South Carolina Culinary History

You can taste a bit of South Carolina culinary history with this recipe. Adluh Flour Mills produces flour and cornmeal products in a plant that is listed on the National Register of Historic Properties. Adluh Flour Mills began in Columbia around 1900. In 1942 there were 42 operating mills located in the state. Adluh Flour Mills in Columbia, South Carolina is the only remaining mill operating today. This recipe uses Adluh Yellow Flake Biscuit Mix which is a complete biscuit mix blended from enriched soft wheat flour. It is easy to use since only water, milk or buttermilk must be added, and can be used in a variety of recipes such as buttermilk biscuits, pancakes, waffles, cobblers, and even pot pies.

Oatmeal Raisin Breakfast Mini Muffins

½ cup raisins
½ cup flour
½ cup quick oats
½ cup sugar
1 teaspoon cinnamon
1 teaspoon baking powder
¼ teaspoon baking soda
¼ teaspoon salt
1 egg, lightly beaten
¾ cup low-fat vanilla yogurt
2 tablespoons canola oil
1 teaspoon vanilla

Victoria Rayu/istock/thinkstock

Preheat oven to 400°. Coat mini muffin tin with nonstick cooking spray. In large bowl, combine raisins, flour, oats, sugar, cinnamon, baking powder, baking soda and salt; set aside. In separate bowl, combine egg, yogurt, oil and vanilla, mixing well with a whisk. Add to dry ingredients and stir until just moistened. Divide equal portions into prepared mini muffin tin and bake 12 to 14 minutes or until wooden pick inserted comes out clean. Cool on rack. Yields 24 mini muffins.

Peach Morning Muffins

2 cups finely chopped fresh South Carolina peaches
1½ cups sugar, divided
1 stick (½ cup) butter, softened
2 eggs
4 cups flour, divided
4 teaspoons baking powder
1 teaspoon salt
1½ cups milk
¼ cup brown sugar
¼ cup ground pecans
¼ teaspoon cinnamon
4 tablespoons cold butter

A warm muffin is a filling way to start the day. Actually, these muffins are great anytime of the day. This recipe makes for a flavor-filled muffin with a hint of cinnamon along with the delicious combination of South Carolina peaches and brown sugar.

Preheat oven to 400°. Lightly grease 24 muffin cups. Place peaches in a bowl and cover with ½ cup sugar. Mix thoroughly. Allow peaches to sit 1 hour. Using an electric mixer, cream 1 stick butter and remaining 1 cup sugar until smooth and pale in color, about 3 minutes. Add eggs, 1 at a time, and beat until fluffy, about 2 minutes. In a separate bowl, combine 3½ cups flour, baking powder and salt. By hand, alternately fold in milk and flour mixture, being careful not to overmix. Fold in peaches. Spoon ¼ cup batter into each prepared muffin cup.

In a small bowl, combine remaining ½ cup flour, brown sugar, pecans and cinnamon. Mix well. Add 4 tablespoons cold butter. Using your hands, mix until mixture resembles coarse crumb-like mixture. Sprinkle 1 teaspoon crumb mixture over batter in each muffin cup. Bake 15 to 20 minutes or until golden brown. Serve warm with butter.

South Carolina Peach Council

Fig Preserves

2 cups fresh figs
1 cup sugar

Wash figs and remove stems. Combine with sugar in saucepan, and simmer until desired thickness. Pack into sterilized jars; seal with sterilized lids. Keep refrigerated or process in water bath for 10 minutes.

South Carolina Department of Agriculture

Peanut Butter Muffins

2 cups sifted all-purpose flour
1 tablespoon baking powder
1 cup milk
2 eggs
½ cup sugar

½ cup creamy peanut butter
1 teaspoon salt
1 cup chopped peanuts plus more for topping, if desired

Preheat oven to 400°. Combine flour and baking powder; set aside. Place milk, eggs, sugar, peanut butter and salt in blender container; cover and blend. Combine dry ingredients, peanut butter mixture and chopped peanuts. Top with additional peanuts, if desired. Fill greased muffin pans ⅔ full. Top with additional peanuts, if desired. Bake 15 to 20 minutes, or until a toothpick inserted into the center comes out clean. Makes 12.

Warren Price/istock/thinkstock

Plantation Rice Muffins

2 cups flour
4 teaspoons baking powder
½ teaspoon salt
1 cup cold cooked rice

1 cup milk
2 eggs, well-beaten
3 tablespoons melted butter

Preheat oven to 425°. Sift flour, baking powder and salt. Stir in rice. In a separate bowl, combine milk and eggs; add to dry ingredients and mix well. Stir in butter. Fill well-greased muffin tins ½ full and bake 25 minutes. Makes 12 muffins.

Kiwifruit Bread

4 kiwifruit
¾ cup sugar
½ cup margarine, softened
2 eggs
½ cup halved red candied cherries

2¼ cups sifted flour
3 teaspoons baking powder
1 teaspoon baking soda
½ teaspoon salt

Peel and dice kiwifruit. Place in saucepan and cook over medium-low heat with a small amount of water until heated thoroughly. Add enough water to make 1¼ cups fruit and cool. Beat sugar and margarine together; blend in eggs. Stir cooled kiwifruit and cherries into sugar mixture. Sift dry ingredients together. Blend dry ingredients into kiwifruit mixture. Pour batter into well-oiled and floured 9x5-inch loaf pan. Bake at 350° for 1 hour or until bread tests done. Cool in pan 5 minutes; invert onto wire rack. Slice thin to serve. (Bread slices better the day after it is baked.) Yields 1 loaf.

South Carolina Department of Agriculture

Pumpkin Bread

1½ cups sugar
1 cup cooked or canned pumpkin
½ cup vegetable oil
½ cup water
2 eggs
1⅔ cups flour
1 teaspoon baking soda

1 teaspoon cinnamon
¾ teaspoon salt
½ teaspoon baking powder
½ teaspoon ground nutmeg
¼ teaspoon ground cloves
½ cup chopped walnuts (optional)
½ cup raisins (optional)

In mixing bowl, combine sugar, pumpkin, oil, water and eggs; beat well. In a separate bowl, combine flour, baking soda, cinnamon, salt, baking powder, nutmeg and cloves. Gradually add dry mixture to pumpkin mixture and mix well. Stir in nuts and raisins, if desired. Pour into greased 9x5-inch loaf pan. Bake at 350° for 65 to 70 minutes or until bread tests done. Cool in pan 10 minutes, then turn bread out and cool on wire rack.

South Carolina Department of Agriculture

May River

"Old Timey" Peach Bread

**2 cups mashed South Carolina peaches
    (1½ pounds very ripe fresh peaches)
1 large egg, slightly beaten
2 tablespoons melted butter
½ cup raisins or sliced almonds
2 cups flour
½ cup sugar
½ cup firmly packed brown sugar
1 teaspoon baking soda
⅛ teaspoon salt**

Drain peaches. In a bowl, combine peaches with beaten egg and melted butter. Stir in raisins or almonds. In a separate bowl, mix together flour, sugars, baking soda and salt. Add flour mixture to peach mixture, combining well. Pour batter into greased and floured 9x5-inch loaf pan. Let stand 20 minutes. Bake at 350° for 45 to 55 minutes. Cool in pan 15 minutes and finish cooling on wire rack. Drizzle with Glaze.

Glaze:

**1 cup powdered sugar
2 teaspoons lemon juice**

Mix together ingredients. Add more juice if necessary. Drizzle over cooled peach bread.

South Carolina Peach Council

South Carolina Peach Festival
Gaffney • 3rd Weekend in July

The South Carolina Peach Festival includes a sanctioned BBQ cook-off, parade, sanctioned 5K & 10K road race, arts & crafts, food vendors, live concerts, cornhole tournament, golf tournament, peach dessert contest, carnival rides, mud bog and more!! This is one festival you don't want to miss!

864.489.5716 • www.scpeachfestival.org

Dawn's Monkey Bread

3 (10-count) cans biscuits
3 teaspoons cinnamon, divided
1¾ cups sugar, divided
1 stick (½ cup) butter or margarine

Preheat oven to 350°. Cut biscuits into fourths. Mix 1 teaspoon cinnamon and ¾ cup sugar in a bowl or a large zip-close bag. Coat biscuit pieces, a few at a time, in mixture until well coated. Place biscuit pieces in a nonstick Bundt pan (or grease the pan). Sprinkle any remaining sugar/cinnamon mixture on top. Melt butter with remaining 2 teaspoons cinnamon and 1 cup sugar (sugar won't fully dissolve). Spoon or pour evenly over biscuits. Refrigerate to bake later or bake at 350° for 35 minutes. Remove from oven and let cool about 20 minutes (unless you can't keep from diving in). Turn bread out onto a plate or serving tray. Enjoy.

This recipe was given to me back in 1985 when I was the skating director at Stone Mountain Ice Chalet. A dear old friend of mine named Barbara Garrett wrote it on the back of a handout for a ladies Bible study. Barbara used to make it for the judges to enjoy in the hospitality room at all of our skating competitions. Now it has been the standard EVERY Christmas morning at my home, and is one of my traditions that I truly adore! Nothing says a "Southern" Christmas like monkey bread right out of the oven, a cup of coffee, a mimosa or Bloody Mary, and then checking the stockings!

Dawn Malone Goldys, Charleston

Heather's Stuffed Apple-Cinnamon Rolls

1 (13.8-ounce) can refrigerated pizza dough
2 cups shredded green apples (2 to 3 large apples)
3 tablespoons brown sugar
1¼ teaspoons cinnamon, divided

1 tablespoon flour
2 tablespoons melted butter, divided
1 tablespoon sugar
6 tablespoons powdered sugar
¼ teaspoon vanilla or almond extract
1 to 2 teaspoons milk

Preheat oven to temperature specified on pizza dough package. Coat pie plate or similar dish with nonstick cooking spray; set aside. On a lightly floured surface, roll pizza dough into a rectangle approximately 12x18 inches. Using a pizza cutter, cut dough into 3-inch squares, making 10 to 15 squares. In a bowl, combine apples, brown sugar, 1 teaspoon cinnamon and flour. Place a spoonful of apple mixture on each square of dough. To seal each square, wrap dough around filling and pinch to seal, forming a round ball. Place seam side down in pie plate. Combine 1 tablespoon melted butter, sugar and ¼ teaspoon cinnamon; brush mixture on each ball. Bake 15 to 20 minutes or until rolls are golden brown. Remove from oven and cool 10 minutes. While rolls are cooling, combine powdered sugar, remaining 1 tablespoon melted butter, vanilla and milk; whisk until smooth. Drizzle on rolls and serve.

Heather Steele, Charleston
The Navy Wives of South Carolina Recipes

Blueberry French Toast Baked Betty

½-inch-thick French bread slices (enough to fill bottom of baking dish)
5 eggs
2½ cups milk
1 cup packed brown sugar, divided
2 teaspoons vanilla
2 teaspoons cinnamon
½ teaspoon ground nutmeg
1 cup chopped pecans
¼ cup butter or margarine, melted
2 cups fresh or frozen blueberries

Arrange French bread in a well-greased 9x13-inch glass baking dish (do not use a metal dish). In a bowl, combine eggs, milk, ¾ cup brown sugar, vanilla, cinnamon and nutmeg; pour over bread. Cover and refrigerate 8 hours or overnight. Remove from refrigerator about 30 minutes before baking. Preheat oven to 400°. Sprinkle pecans over top. Combine melted butter and remaining ¼ cup sugar; drizzle over top. Bake, uncovered, for 25 minutes. Sprinkle with blueberries. Bake 10 minutes longer or until a knife inserted near the center comes out clean.

Cypress Gardens, Moncks Corner

Andrea Pelletier/istock/thinkstock

Kent's Real Beignets & Cheater Beignets

1 (¼-ounce) package active dry yeast
¼ cup warm water (110° to 115°)
1 cup evaporated milk (not condensed)
½ cup canola oil
¼ cup sugar
1 egg
4½ cups self-rising flour, divided
Oil for deep frying
Powdered sugar

First, note that this recipe does use both yeast and self-rising flour, you did not read that wrong. Secondly, this recipe rises overnight, so keep that in mind when figuring your cooking times. And lastly, use evaporated milk, not condensed milk.

In a large bowl, dissolve yeast in warm water. Add milk, oil, sugar, egg and 2 cups flour. Beat until mixture is smooth. Stir in enough remaining flour to form a soft dough (dough will be sticky). Do not knead the dough at this time. Cover and refrigerate overnight.

Next day, uncover the dough and punch down. Turn onto a floured surface and gently roll into a 12x16-inch rectangle. Cut into 2-inch squares. In an electric skillet or deep fryer, heat oil to 375°. Fry the squares until golden brown on both sides. Flip as needed, sometimes they flip on their own. Only cook a few at a time, this helps them evenly cook and maintains the heat of the oil. Drain on paper towels. Roll warm beignets in powdered sugar.

For the Cheaters Version:

Refrigerated bread sticks (can be found next to canned biscuits)
Powdered sugar

Cut bread sticks into 1-inch long pieces. Fry in hot oil until golden. Drain and sprinkle with powdered sugar.

Fresh Apple Croissants

2 tablespoons sugar
1 teaspoon cinnamon
1 (8-ounce) can crescent rolls

1 large cooking apple, peeled and cut
into slices

Preheat oven to 375°. In a small bowl, combine sugar and cinnamon. Separate dough into triangles and sprinkle with sugar mixture. Place a few apple slices on each triangle. Roll up and pinch ends together of each crescent. Bake at 375° for 15 to 20 minutes.

South Carolina Department of Agriculture

Davide Chiarito/istock/thinkstock

Breakfast Shrimp and Grits

1 pound shrimp, shelled and deveined
Butter
Salt
Parsley
4 cups hot, cooked grits

Sauté shrimp in butter until done. Add a pinch of salt and sprinkle with parsley. Serve over grits in a bowl.

Shrimp and grits was traditionally eaten for breakfast by coastal fishermen and their families. Not just for breakfast anymore, shrimp and grits has been adapted for lunch and dinner and is now served even in fine dining restaurants. This basic recipe gets back to the tradition of shrimp and grits for breakfast.

World Grits Festival
Saint George • April

The objective of the grits festival is to stimulate pride in the town of St. George and surrounding communities and to provide wholesome recreation and entertainment for the entire family. Activities are unlimited for all ages, such as rolling in the grits, 5K run, corn toss, grits eating, grits grinding, grits meals, corn shelling, parade, carnival, food booths, grits sampling, corn shelling, and much more.

843.563.7943
www.worldgritsfestival.com

Shrimp Soufflé Breakfast

18 slices bread, crusts removed
4 cups partially cooked shrimp
2½ cups grated sharp Cheddar cheese
　(or Cheddar-Jack blend)
8 eggs, beaten
3 cups half-and-half
1 teaspoon salt
1 teaspoon dry mustard
1 teaspoon lemon pepper
½ cup crushed Ritz-style crackers
½ cup butter

My family owns Independent Seafood in Georgetown and we have been serving up local, wild caught American shrimp to guests since 1937. Needless to say...shrimp for breakfast is our specialty! I often serve guests this soufflé with seasoned Italian sausage patties, fresh tomatoes and cucumbers in a sour cream-dill sauce and poached pears. A great addition to the menu is fresh bread and pastries from Kudzu Bakery right here in town, a local favorite.

Place 9 slices of bread in 9x13-inch greased baking pan. Sprinkle with shrimp and cheese. Top with remaining bread slices. Combine eggs, half-and-half, salt, dry mustard and lemon pepper in a bowl; evenly pour over layers. Cover and chill overnight in fridge. Mix crushed crackers and butter and sprinkle over top of casserole right before baking. Bake uncovered at 350° for 1 hour until set and cooked in the middle; a few more minutes may be needed. Serves 10 to 12. You can halve it for a smaller version to serve 4 to 6.

Meg Tarbox, Georgetown

Brunch Casserole

1 egg
2 tablespoons milk
1 (8-count) can Pillsbury Grands biscuits
1 cup shredded Cheddar cheese
4 to 6 slices bacon, fried crisp and crumbled (or 4 to 6 tablespoons Real
    bacon bits)
¼ to ⅓ cup finely grated onion

Beat egg and milk together. Quarter biscuits. Place in egg mixture, turning to coat. Add cheese, bacon and onion to biscuits and egg mixture. Pour into greased 9x13-inch baking dish. Bake at 350° for 25 to 30 minutes.

Catherine Murray/istock/thinkstock

Fruit Pizza

Crust:

1 (16.5-ounce) package refrigerated
    sugar cookie dough
½ cup sugar

1 (8-ounce) package cream cheese,
    softened
1 teaspoon vanilla

Spread cookie dough on lightly greased pizza pan. Bake in 350° oven for 10 minutes. Mix sugar, cream cheese and vanilla. Spread over cooled cookie crust.

Fruit:

Strawberries, sliced or whole
Peach slices
Blueberries
Pineapple slices

Raspberries
Banana slices
Grapes, halved
Blackberries

Place your preference of fruit on top of crust.

Topping:

¾ cup sugar
1 cup orange juice
¼ cup lemon juice

¾ cup water
3 tablespoons cornstarch

Combine sugar, orange juice, lemon juice, water and cornstarch. Bring to a boil and cook 1 minute. Cool and spoon over fruit. Be sure to cover fruit. Chill, cut and serve.

South Carolina Department of Agriculture

Jessica's "Cheeze" Toast Pizza

Shredded Cheddar, Romano or provolone
    cheese, your choice
Bread slices (any kind you like)
Cherry tomatoes or sun-dried tomatoes, sliced
Basil
Italian breadcrumbs

Jessica, my youngest, loves to get creative in the kitchen. She makes this quick recipe when she is pressed for time.

Preheat oven to 400°. Place a generous amount of cheese on each slice of bread. Top with tomatoes, then sprinkle with basil. Sprinkle Italian breadcrumbs on top of everything. Bake until brown and bubbly. It's 10 minutes to heaven for a quick lunch.

Sally Morris, Greenwood
www.RealEstateGreenwoodSC.com

Alysa's Quick and Easy BLT Pizza

1 (13.8-ounce) can refrigerated pizza
    dough
1 pound bacon
1 (16-ounce) bag shredded cheese

1 head iceburg lettuce, shredded
4 tablespoons mayonnaise
1 large tomato, sliced and cut in half
    (semi-circles)

Preheat oven to 325°. Roll pizza dough onto a pizza pan and set aside. Cook bacon until half done (see tip below) and place pieces on pizza dough; top with cheese and bake 15 minutes. Toss shredded lettuce with mayonnaise until thoroughly coated. When pizza is done baking, slice as desired. Spoon lettuce onto each slice and top with tomato.

Quick Tip: To cook the bacon halfway in your microwave, place 5 pieces between 2 paper towels and cook 2 minutes. That equals about 1 minute for every 2½ pieces.

Alysa Schnepf, Charleston
The Navy Wives of South Carolina Recipes

Soups & Salads

**Fish Muddle,
page 59**

Bacon and Blackened Okra Soup with Carolina Rice

30 to 40 okra, cleaned, stemmed and chopped
Olive oil
2 sweet onions, chopped fine
2 tablespoons butter
2 tablespoons parsley flakes
½ tablespoon thyme
¼ tablespoon garlic powder
½ red bell pepper, chopped
2 (14.5-ounce) cans diced tomatoes
1 beef bouillon cube
1 to 1½ cups cooked crumbled bacon
3½ quarts hot water
1 tablespoon creole seasoning
Salt and pepper to taste

You can use frozen okra, but I prefer as fresh as possible. One time I sent my husband to the store for okra and he bought frozen BREADED okra! I was a bit mad but laughed as well. He didn't even look at the bag. So...we tried it in the soup. It was not too bad, but I probably won't make that version of the recipe again! We have made this recipe using leftover ham in place of the bacon. And once I used blackened whole-kernel corn instead of okra. They were all good!

Very lightly coat okra with oil. Place on cookie sheet and broil until okra begins to blacken, turning frequently. Be careful not to allow okra to burn and dry out. If using frozen okra, thaw completely before broiling. In a skillet, sauté onions in butter with parsley, thyme and garlic powder. When onions are golden brown, add onions, okra and remaining ingredients to a large pot; cover. Simmer on low for about 1 hour; add additional seasonings, if needed. Serve hot over cooked South Carolina rice with a slice of hot toasted French bread.

Karen Burns, Charleston

Okra Soup

1 soup bone
1½ pounds stew beef
1½ quarts water
1 (28-ounce) can tomatoes
1 cup butter beans (or green limas)
3 cups sliced fresh okra
1 large onion, chopped
Salt and pepper to taste

Boil soup bone and beef in water for 2 hours. Add remaining ingredients and cook over medium heat about 1 hour adding more water if necessary.

South Carolina Department of Parks, Recreation & Tourism

Irmo Okra Strut Festival
Irmo • Last Weekend in September

The Irmo Okra Strut Festival will be celebrating its 41st anniversary in 2014. The festival runs from 6:00 p.m. until 11:00 p.m. Friday night with the Street Dance beginning at 7:00 p.m. There will be lots of entertainment, food, amusements, and our famous Okra Eating Contest. The festival site is open from 10:00 a.m. until 5:00 p.m. on Saturday. Beginning at 9:20 Saturday we will feature the largest festival parade in South Carolina featuring over 100 entries. After watching the parade, please join us for plenty of food, amusements, and entertainment as well as 100 artists and crafters from across the Southeast. Of course the Irmo-Lake Murray Women's Club will be featuring their famous "Fried Okra" Friday night and all day Saturday.

803.661.1049 • www.irmookrastrut.com

Brooke Elizabeth Becker/istock/thinkstock

kabVisio/istock/thinkstock

Folly Beach Onion Soup

10 (12-ounce) cans cold Budweiser Beer
10 medium Vidalia onions
6 bouillon cubes
6 tablespoons Worcestershire sauce
4 tablespoons Dale's Steak Seasoning
3 tablespoons fresh ground pepper
1 pound Gruyere cheese, sliced
1 fresh baked baguette

This dish is guaranteed to warm the soul after a spring surf session or to clear the mind after a good evening on Center Street. I named it after one of my favorite places to surf—Folly Beach. It feeds about eight people and takes about two hours to prepare. I use Vidalia onions whenever possible, but you can substitute any sweet onion. Remember, onions are seasonal and different in variety, so you may have to tweak your recipe a bit to dial your taste in. Enjoy.

In a large stockpot, combine all ingredients, except cheese and bread. Bring to a slow boil, stirring occasionally. Initially all onions will be floating and soup will have a strong oniony bitter taste. But, don't worry. The onions are just releasing their flavors. As the onions cook they will become transparent and the flavor will mellow as the beer and other ingredients mingle. When onions begin to sink, reduce heat to a simmer. Taste-test and add Worcestershire (sweet), Dale's (salty), and pepper (spicy). You are looking for a slightly salty, mellow onion flavor with a hint of sweet, backed by a surprise beer bitter finish. Once you are satisfied with the taste, spoon into oven-safe bowls leaving about 1 inch at the top. Cover each bowl with 1-inch slices of the baguette. Top with 1 to 2 slices of Gruyere cheese and broil until cheese bubbles and turns a golden brown. Serve hot with remaining baguette and your favorite beer or wine.

David Tomblin, The Tomblin Company, Charleston

Roasted Butternut Squash and Vidalia Bisque

This is a good example of my cooking style— Classic French with a Southern flair—derived from my family, French immigrants and generations of South Carolinians.

Roasted Squash:

½ cup unsalted butter
1 large butternut squash, peeled, halved, seeded and cubed
1 large Vidalia onion, large dice
1 tablespoon kosher salt
1 teaspoon ground coriander
1 teaspoon cinnamon

1 teaspoon ground cardamom
1 teaspoon chili powder
1 teaspoon pepper flakes
½ teaspoon mace
¼ cup balsamic vinegar
½ cup molasses

In large skillet, brown butter over high heat until slightly brown; add squash and onion. Toss. Add dry spices, and toss again. Add balsamic vinegar and molasses, and toss. Place on baking sheet, and bake at 375° for 15 minutes or until squash is fork tender. Set aside to cool.

Bisque:

3 to 4 cups chicken stock (preferably simmered with mirepoix blend)

1 cup half-and-half
Salt to taste

In food processor or blender, purée Roasted Squash with 2 cups chicken stock and half-and-half. Add additional stock until a slightly thick consistency is achieved. Add salt to taste.

Geoffrey D. Sandifer, Governor's Mansion Executive Chef

Stillwater Vanilla Cucumber Soup

5 ounces sour cream
1 (12-ounce) bottle Stillwater Vanilla
   Cream Ale
1 large cucumber, peeled and diced
1 clove garlic, peeled and finely diced
Salt and pepper to taste
1 teaspoon paprika (optional)
Mint leaves for garnish (optional)

Mix sour cream and Stillwater Vanilla Cream Ale until an even consistency is achieved. Toss together cucumber and garlic in separate bowl; then add to sour cream and ale mixture. Season with salt and pepper. Cover and chill at least 1 hour. Just before serving, I like adding a few dashes of paprika and a few mint leaves as garnish, for an appealing presentation. Serve chilled and enjoy!

Christopher McElveen
Thomas Creek Brewery, Greenville

Make it ahead of time to let the flavors mix. I use our Thomas Creek Brewery Stillwater Vanilla Cream Ale but you can use your favorite cream ale.

Falls Creek Falls, Mountain Bridge Wilderness Area, Greenville County

Sweet Potato Soup

2 cups mashed sweet potatoes
1½ cups chicken or turkey broth
1 cup heavy cream or half-and-half

Salt to taste
White pepper to taste
Ground nutmeg to taste

In blender, purée sweet potatoes, broth and cream until smooth. Transfer to saucepan; heat over low heat. Season to taste with salt, white pepper and nutmeg. Yields 4 to 6 servings.

Janice Kara, McColl

Hilton Head Island Seafood Fest
Hilton Head Island • April

The Hilton Head Island Seafood Fest, which takes place annually in April at the Shelter Cove Community Park, is sponsored by the David M. Carmines Memorial Foundation and Hilton Head Chrysler Dodge Jeep Ram. It helps raise money for the American Cancer Society, MD Anderson Cancer Research Center & Island Recreation Scholarship Fund. The two day, family-friendly event features area restaurants/chefs serving up seafood specialties and other tasty cuisine, live entertainment, a Kids Zone, a silent auction, an Iron Chef-style competition (Art of Cuisine), and more.

843.681.7273 • www.davidmcarmines.org

Amber Cheese Soup

2 tablespoons olive oil
1 medium red onion, diced
2 cloves garlic, minced
2 celery stalks, diced
2 carrots, diced
⅓ cup all-purpose flour
2 cups chicken broth
2 cups milk

1 (12-ounce) bottle Appalachian
   Amber Ale
16 ounces shredded Cheddar cheese,
   divided
Salt and pepper to taste
Chopped bacon for garnish (optional)
Chopped chives for garnish (optional)

Heat olive oil in large pan over medium-high heat. Add onion and garlic; cook 3 to 5 minutes. Reduce heat to medium and add celery and carrots. Continue cooking 6 to 8 minutes until vegetables are soft. Add flour to pan and mix until evenly distributed and all liquid is absorbed. Stir in chicken broth, then add milk and Appalachian Amber Ale. Stir until all liquid is incorporated and continue cooking until foam from beer subsides and soup begins to thicken, about 5 minutes. Reduce heat to simmer and slowly add 10 ounces Cheddar cheese, stirring constantly. Continue simmering 10 to 15 minutes. Season to taste and garnish with remaining 6 ounces shredded cheese, bacon or chives.

*Christopher McElveen,
Thomas Creek Brewery, Greenville*

Azurita/istock/thinkstock

Lowcountry Clam Chowder

**2 pounds fresh clams, shelled, or 1 pound
    shelled or canned clams**
4 to 5 slices bacon, diced
1 medium onion, chopped
6 medium potatoes, peeled and cubed
4 cups milk
Salt and pepper to taste
1 cup light cream
1 tablespoon flour
Chopped parsley (optional)

*We make this clam chowder when we
want to feel like we are at the beach.
I use fresh South Carolina clams
whenever I can. But, in a pinch, canned
clams will do. This uses a lot of clams so
adjust your milk as needed.*

Drain clams, reserving juice. Set both aside. Sauté bacon until fat is rendered. Remove bacon and set aside. Add onions to pan and cook until softened. Add potatoes, milk, reserved clam juice, salt and pepper. Cover and boil 12 minutes or until potatoes are tender. Whisk cream and flour until smooth. Add to pot with clams and bacon. Heat through without letting chowder come to a boil. Serve hot with garnish of parsley.

Kassandra Britt DeFranco, Greenville

Daniel Padavona/istock/thinkstock

She-Crab Soup

You don't need to scurry around for She-Crab Soup, because just about every Lowcountry restaurant in South Carolina offers their variation on this wonderfully appetizing dish that may be at its best when enjoyed on a chilly afternoon. According to the *South Carolina Encyclopedia*, She-Crab Soup is described as "a silky, seafood chowder with a European heritage." Food historians believe that originally she-crab soup was a seafood bisque brought to the New World in the early 1700s by Scottish settlers. The signature dish of Charleston, the soup is named for the "She Crab," or female crab, which supplies the flavorful orange roe, or eggs, that are a chief ingredient in the soup. A blending of New and Old Worlds and served hot, She-Crab Soup is often garnished with a sprinkling of the orange crab eggs and by a dollop of a fine, dry sherry.

82 Queen's She-Crab Soup

1 cup chopped celery
¼ cup chopped carrots
¼ cup chopped onion
1 stick plus 2 tablespoons butter, divided
½ cup flour
3 cups milk
1 cup heavy cream
2 cups fish stock or water and fish base
¼ pound crab roe
1 pound white crabmeat
¼ cup sherry wine
1 tablespoon Tabasco Sauce
1 tablespoon Worcestershire sauce

This delicious recipe for She-Crab Soup is served in Charleston's most historic restaurant, 82 Queen. Dating back to 1688 when South Carolina was a newly formed colony, the three buildings known as 82 Queen Street are located on the site of the former Schenckingh's Square, once part of the original walled city of Charles Towne. Since 1982, 82 Queen has been providing its guests with gracious Southern hospitality, award-winning wines and authentic fresh Lowcountry cuisine.

Lightly sauté celery, carrots and onion in 2 tablespoons butter. In a separate pot, melt remaining 1 stick butter; stir in flour to make a roux. Whisk in milk and cream until smooth. Bring to a boil. Add sautéed vegetables and remaining ingredients; simmer 20 minutes. Garnish with sherried whipped cream.

82 Queen Restaurant, Charleston
South Carolina Department of Parks, Recreation & Tourism

Easy Lowcountry Cream Soup with Shrimp or Crab

½ cup chopped red bell pepper
¼ cup minced onion
3 (10¾-ounce) cans cream of mushroom
    soup
2 cups milk
½ cup sour cream
1 chicken bouillon cube
Dash Old Bay seafood seasoning
2 cups cooked salad shrimp or crabmeat

This is a quick version of a recipe that my mom used to make. This will feed a family of four, and you can stretch it by adding more milk or cream. It makes canned soup taste more like homemade.

Combine all ingredients, except shrimp or crabmeat, in a medium pot. Cook over medium heat until onions and peppers are soft. Add shrimp or crabmeat towards the end of cooking time to heat. Don't over-stir because the meat will break up. Serve hot in a bowl topped with parsley flakes, paprika and large croutons.

Miss B., Beaufort

razmarinka/istock/thinkstock

Fish Muddle

2 tablespoons vegetable oil
2 large onions, sliced or chopped
2 carrots, chopped
2 celery stalks, thinly sliced
1 clove garlic, minced
1 (14.4-ounce) can diced tomatoes, drained
2 to 3 medium potatoes, chopped small
5 to 6 cups fish stock or bottled clam juice
Salt and pepper to taste
12 small clams, scrubbed (or canned)
1 pound fish (your choice), cut into pieces
½ pound medium shrimp, peeled and deveined
12 small mussels, rinsed and beards removed*
¼ cup finely chopped fresh parsley

Some call this fish muddle, some call it seafood muddle, and others call it just plain old muddle. So...what is muddle? Muddle is dish that is very similar to a seafood stew. When you have a whole lot of fish, they became a "muddle" of fish stew.

Heat oil in a large soup pot over medium-high heat. Add onions, carrots and celery. Cook until softened, 3 to 5 minutes, stirring often. Add garlic and cook 1 minute longer. Stir in tomatoes and potatoes. Reduce heat to medium-low, cover and cook until potatoes are slightly softened, about 10 minutes. Pour in fish stock and increase heat to high. Bring to a boil, reduce heat to medium, and season with salt and pepper. Simmer until potatoes are completely cooked, 10 to 15 minutes longer. Add clams and cook until they start to open, about 5 minutes. Add fish, shrimp and mussels. Cook about 10 minutes longer until fish is opaque, shrimp are pink, and clams and mussels are fully opened. Discard any clams or mussels that remain unopened. Season again with salt and pepper, sprinkle with parsley and serve hot.

*Mussels can be replaced with additional shrimp or fish.

Hearty Oyster Stew

2 pints small, fresh Bluffton oysters
2 cups chicken broth, divided, or more
as needed
2 cups peeled and ¼-inch-diced
potatoes
½ cup peeled and ¼-inch-diced Vidalia
or Spanish onion
½ cup washed well, cut in half and
sliced leek
¼ cup white celery, tiny inner stalks
minced

1 teaspoon minced garlic
2 bay leaves
2 tablespoons butter
1 cup water
½ cup French vermouth or dry white
drinking wine
1 cup half-and-half
1 teaspoon hot pepper sauce
Salt to taste
2 tablespoons minced fresh chives

Drain oysters, reserving liquid. Combine liquid with enough chicken broth to make 2 cups (reserving remaining chicken broth); set aside. In a large soup pot over medium heat, add potatoes, onion, leek, celery, garlic, bay leaves, butter, water and 1 cup chicken broth. Cover and gently simmer about 10 minutes to combine flavors. Do not brown; lower heat if necessary. Add reserved 2 cups oyster liquid and wine. Continue simmering another 15 minutes until potatoes are very soft. Remove bay leaves. Add half-and-half and hot pepper sauce. In a separate medium saucepan, heat oysters just until edges curl. Stir oysters and accumulated juices into stew. Sprinkle with chives and stir.

South Carolina Department of Parks, Recreation & Tourism

Lowcountry Oyster Festival
Mount Pleasant • January

The Charleston Restaurant Association hosts the annual Lowcountry Oyster Festival on the 500+ acre grounds of historic Boone Hall Plantation in Mount Pleasant. The Lowcountry Oyster Festival is the world's largest oyster roast and has been named one of the "top 20 events in the Southeast" by the Southeastern Tourism Society. More than 10,000 guests are expected and 65,000 pounds of oysters served throughout the day on the back lawn of the plantation. Other highlights include the legendary Oyster Shucking and Oyster Eating contests, a selection of domestic and imported beers, live music on the main stage and a Children's Area. For those who are not so keen on the mighty mollusk, there will be a Food Court with alternate food selections.

843.577.4030
www.charlestonrestaurantassociation.com

7 Can Brunswick Stew

2 (15-ounce) cans BBQ chicken
2 (15-ounce) cans BBQ pork
2 (14.5-ounce) cans diced tomatoes
1 (11-ounce) can whole-kernel corn
2 tablespoons minced onions
1 teaspoon chili powder
Hot sauce to taste
Salt and pepper to taste

Combine all ingredients in a slow cooker, stir, and cook on low 3 to 4 hours. Then receive praise from your family and friends for the "best Brunswick stew" they've ever had. Works wonderfully for a potluck. Enjoy!

Kelly Watson, Aiken

Lowcountry Catfish Stew

5 pounds cleaned catfish
1½ pounds pork fatback
5 pounds onions, chopped
5 pounds potatoes, chopped
4 (14.5-ounce) cans diced tomatoes
1 (10-ounce) can tomato purée
1 (6-ounce) can tomato paste
1 tablespoon red pepper flakes
1 tablespoon black pepper
Salt to taste

Place catfish in water to cover and bring to a boil. When cooked, strain out fish, reserving water. Pick meat from bones; discard bones and any other unwanted pieces. Slice pork fatback and cut into small pieces. Fry in a large stockpot; do not fry crisp. Add reserved water, chopped onions and potatoes, tomatoes, tomato purée, tomato paste, red and black peppers, and salt to pot. Bring to a boil, then simmer 2½ hours. Stir frequently, so stew doesn't stick to bottom of pot. Add catfish during last half hour, just to heat.

Manager Mike Hicks
and the hometown employees
Southeastern Salvage, Columbia

Ware Shoals Catfish Feastival
Ware Shoals • Memorial Day Weekend

Ware Shoals Catfish "Feastival" is a time of fun entertainment, arts & crafts, carnival rides, a special children's program, classic car show, and delicious food. It's also a time of hospitality as we welcome former residents, guests, and tourists. With great family fun for everyone to go along with catfish stew, fried catfish, plus fried and barbecue chicken, we encourage you to feast away at our Feastival!

864.554.7024 • www.CatfishFeastival.com

Danny Hooks/istock/thinkstock

Pumphouse Porter Irish Stew

2 tablespoons butter
2 pounds lamb, cubed
1 large onion, chopped
2 carrots, chopped
3 potatoes, cubed
1 cup beef stock
2 tablespoons tomato purée
1 teaspoon sugar
1 (12-ounce) bottle Pumphouse Porter
1 teaspoon parsley
1 teaspoon thyme
1 bay leaf
Salt and pepper to taste

If you can't get your hands on our Thomas Creek Brewery Pumphouse Porter made right here in South Carolina, then try one of your favorite porters. This is a great recipe for a hearty Irish stew!

In a Dutch oven, melt butter and brown lamb over medium-high heat. Remove lamb from pan and allow to rest. Add onion and carrots to pan, cook until slightly softened. Add lamb back to pan along with potatoes, beef stock, tomato purée and sugar. Bring to a boil, then reduce heat to a simmer. Stir in Pumphouse Porter, parsley, thyme, bay leaf, salt and pepper. Cook over low heat for 1½ hours, or until lamb is fully cooked and tender. Serve with mashed potatoes or Irish soda bread. Enjoy!

Christopher McElveen
Thomas Creek Brewery, Greenville

South Carolina Chili Day Beef Chili

2½ pounds boneless beef chuck or round, cut into ½-inch pieces
2 (15-ounce) cans black beans, drained and rinsed
1 (15-ounce) can chili-style tomato sauce with diced tomatoes
1 medium onion, chopped
2 teaspoons chili powder
1 teaspoon ground cumin
1 teaspoon salt
½ teaspoon pepper
1 cup prepared thick-and-chunky salsa

South Carolina may be known for Lowcountry food but don't forget the beef! We have many beef producers in the state and that means we have plenty of fantastic beef recipes. Here is one dedicated to National Chili Day, February 25th. We hope this recipe helps warm your heart on a cool February day!

Combine all ingredients, except salsa, in a 4½- to 5½-quart slow cooker; mix well. Cover and cook on high 5½ to 6 hours, or on low 8 to 9 hours, or until beef is tender. (No stirring is necessary during cooking.) Just before serving, stir in salsa; cook 2 to 3 minutes or until heated through. Makes 6 to 8 (1¼- to 1½-cup) servings.

Toppings (optional):

Shredded Cheddar cheese (may use reduced fat, if desired)
Diced onion

Sour cream
Sliced avocado
Sliced green onions

Serve with toppings, if desired.

Roy Copelan, South Carolina Beef Board, Columbia

South Carolina Chili Cook-Off Championship

Belton • 2nd Weekend in April

Sanctioned by the International Chili Society, the South Carolina Chili Cook-Off is one of the Southeast's fastest growing family events. Prizes awarded for Red Chili, Chili Verde, Salsa, Peoples Choice and Showmanship. Proceeds benefit local charities.

864.940.3111 • www.scchilicookoff.com

John's Chili

**3 pounds lean tri-tip, ¼-inch cubes
1¼ cups (10 ounces) chicken broth
1 cup (8 ounces) beef broth
5½ tablespoons hot New Mexico chile powder, divided
2 chicken bouillon cubes
¾ cup (6 ounces) tomato sauce, divided
7 tablespoons mild California chile powder, divided
1 tablespoon garlic powder
1½ tablespoons onion powder
2 teaspoons sea salt, divided
1 tablespoon cumin
2 teaspoons cornstarch**

Rinse meat. Lightly brown in small batches until grey in color. Add to a large stockpot along with chicken broth, beef broth, 2 tablespoons hot chile powder, bouillon cubes and ½ cup tomato sauce. Bring to a boil; cover and reduce to a light boil. Cook 2 hours or until meat is very tender. Add 3 tablespoons hot chile powder, 4 tablespoons mild chile powder, garlic powder, onion powder, 1 teaspoon sea salt and remaining ¼ cup tomato sauce. Lower heat to simmer and cook 30 minutes. Add remaining ½ tablespoon hot chile powder, remaining 3 tablespoons mild chile powder, cumin, cornstarch, and remaining 1 teaspoon sea salt; lower to barely a simmer and cook an additional 30 minutes. Add additional chicken broth as needed.

Inlet Shrimp Salad

1 pound large South Carolina shrimp, peeled and deveined
¼ cup fresh lemon juice
1 small bunch celery, diced
1 medium red onion, diced
1 small bunch green onions, sliced on the bias
1 tablespoon Old Bay seasoning
Kosher salt and ground black pepper to taste
2 cups mayonnaise, more or less to desired consistency

Steam shrimp until just done; do not overcook. Add lemon juice. Chill shrimp while preparing the other ingredients. Combine celery, red onion, green onions, Old Bay seasoning, salt, pepper and mayonnaise. Add mayonnaise mixture to chilled shrimp. Chill until ready to serve. Recipe can easily be halved. Enjoy!

Scott Bishop, Murrells Inlet
South Carolina Department of Parks, Recreation & Tourism

Historic Bluffton Arts & Seafood Festival
Bluffton • October

The annual Historic Bluffton Arts & Seafood Festival is held the third week of October in the charming and eclectic historic district of Bluffton, well known for its quirky art community and natural river beauty. The festival is a week-long event offering a myriad of activities showcasing the locally harvested seafood, delicious Low Country cuisine, rich history, culture and art of the area, and Southern hospitality found only in Bluffton.

The highlight of the festival is the Streetfest which includes a juried fine art show featuring over 100 artists from 10 different states displaying and selling their art, delicious food provided by the area's premier restaurants and caterers, and great music and entertainment on the final weekend of the festival.

Where Fine Art & the Bounty of the Sea Come Together!

843.757.BLUF
www.blufftonartsandseafoodfestival.com

SEWE Shrimp and Pasta Salad

Donna Moulton/istock/thinkstock

1 pound shrimp
1 (16-ounce) package shell or twist pasta
8 ounces fresh mushrooms, sliced
Butter for sautéing
¼ cup olive oil
½ cup red wine vinegar
½ tablespoon garlic salt
1½ tablespoons sugar
1 (1-ounce) packet Italian salad dressing mix
1 (6-ounce) can pitted black olives, drained
1 small onion, thinly sliced

In a saucepan, boil shrimp in water to cover until pink. Drain, reserving the cooking liquid. Peel shrimp. Boil pasta in reserved cooking liquid until al dente; drain. Sauté mushrooms in a small amount of butter in a skillet; drain. Combine olive oil, vinegar, garlic salt, sugar, and salad dressing mix in a bowl and blend well. Combine shrimp, pasta, black olives, onion and sautéed mushrooms in a large bowl. Add the dressing mixture and stir gently to coat. Chill, covered, 3 hours or longer before serving. Yields 6 to 8 servings.

Beth Huggins, VIP Coordinator, Southeastern Wildlife Exposition

South Carolina Grilled Gazpacho Steak Salad

Gazpacho Dressing:

1 (5½-ounce) can spicy 100% vegetable juice
½ cup chopped tomato
¼ cup finely chopped green bell pepper
1 tablespoon red wine vinegar
1 tablespoon chopped cilantro
2 teaspoons olive oil
1 clove garlic, minced

This recipe is amazing in flavor and in ease! It calls for grilling, which gives it a smoky flavor that really is tasty. But when the rain spoils your grilling plans, you can cook the steak indoors in the oven or even in a skillet.

Combine dressing ingredients; refrigerate.

Salad:

1 pound beef top loin strip steak
1 (5½-ounce) can spicy 100% vegetable juice
6 (6-inch) flour tortillas
Salt and pepper to taste
1 cup halved baby pear tomatoes
1 cup thin cucumber slices cut in half
1 cup chopped green bell pepper
8 cups mixed greens or 1 (10-ounce) package romaine and leaf lettuce mixture

Place steak and vegetable juice in zip-close bag; turn steak to coat. Close bag securely and marinate in refrigerator 2 hours.

Meanwhile, prepare crunchy tortilla strips. Cut tortillas into ½-inch-wide strips and scatter on a large baking sheet. Spray with cooking spray and bake at 400° until golden and crisp. Remove from oven and reserve.

Remove steak from marinade; discard marinade. Grill steak over medium, ash-covered coals for 16 to 20 minutes for medium-rare to medium doneness, turning occasionally. Carve steak across the grain into thin slices. Season with salt and pepper.

Combine tomatoes, cucumber, green bell pepper and lettuce. Add steak to salad mixture. Drizzle with Gazpacho Dressing and top with tortilla strips.

Roy Copelan, South Carolina Beef Board, Columbia

Meg's Confetti Chutney Chicken Salad

1 cup mayonnaise
½ cup Major Grey's Chutney
8 boneless, skinless chicken breast halves,
    cooked and cubed
2 stalks celery, chopped
4 green onions, chopped
1 Granny Smith apple, peeled and chopped
½ cup sliced red seedless grapes
½ cup salted cashews

Confetti Chicken Salad was a favorite with our daily lunch crowd when I owned Confetti's Creative Catering and Celebration's, located right on the square in Pendleton. I prefer using chicken breast, but for a wonderful time saver, use a large rotisserie chicken from your favorite grocery store! It's already cooked and many are seasoned for extra flavor. Adding the cashews just before serving keeps them nice and firm for added texture.

Blend mayonnaise and chutney in a bowl. Combine with remaining ingredients, except cashews. Chill 30 minutes to 1 hour. Stir in cashews just before serving.

Meg Tarbox, Georgetown

Twin Falls on Reedy Cove Creek, Eastatoe Valley, Pickens County

John Upchurch/istock/thinkstock

Summer Chicken Salad

1 (12-ounce) package frozen rice pilaf
¼ cup light mayonnaise
¼ cup sour cream or yogurt
1 celery stalk, diced
2 tablespoons sliced green onion
½ teaspoon dried tarragon
¼ teaspoon dried dill weed
Salt and black pepper to taste
2 cups chopped cooked chicken
   (canned or fresh)
4 fresh South Carolina peaches,
   peeled, pitted and sliced
Large lettuce leaves that look like cups

Nothing says summer like chicken salad. This recipe combines all of the savory flavors you would expect from a great serving of chicken salad with the light and fresh taste of a South Carolina peach! A truly amazing combination of flavors.

Prepare rice pilaf according to package directions; cool in mixing bowl. Stir in mayonnaise, sour cream or yogurt, bell pepper, green onion, tarragon, dill weed, salt and pepper. Add chicken; toss lightly to coat. Cover and chill until ready to use. Shortly before serving, add peaches and toss. Serve in lettuce cups.

South Carolina Peach Council

Broccoli Almond Salad

½ cup slivered almonds
6 cups broccoli florets, washed and
    roughly chopped into bite-size pieces
½ cup raisins
¼ cup thinly sliced red onion
3 slices cooked bacon, chopped
1 cup frozen peas (optional)
1 cup mayonnaise
⅓ cup sugar
3 tablespoons red wine vinegar

Place almonds in a dry pan and cook over medium heat 3 to 5 minutes, tossing often. Watch carefully; they will scorch quickly. It is better to under toast. In a large bowl, combine toasted almonds, broccoli, raisins, onion, bacon and peas; set aside. In a separate bowl, combine mayonnaise, sugar and vinegar. Stir briskly until most of the sugar is dissolved. Pour over broccoli mixture and toss, coating well. Cover and chill for 1 hour. Do not skip this step, the flavors need time to marry and broccoli needs time to absorb moisture. Stir before serving.

Heather Solos, Moncks Corner

This is one of those flexible dishes that can be adapted to whatever odds and ends you have in the pantry. Out of slivered almond? Try sunflower seeds. Bacon can be omitted for vegetarians, just increase or add a different type of nut for variety and interest.

Chef Sandifer's "Pimiento Cheese" BLT Salad

1 bag arugula, washed and picked
2 red bell peppers, roasted and cut into strips
½ pound thick-cut bacon, diced and rendered down crispy
2 to 3 heirloom tomatoes, wedged
½ pound shredded Cheddar cheese

Place all ingredients in large bowl and toss well.

Vinaigrette:

1 cup white balsamic vinegar
½ cup buttermilk
½ cup blue cheese crumbles
2 tablespoons minced chives
2 teaspoons black pepper
1 teaspoon salt
1 teaspoon garlic powder

When using heirloom tomatoes, use the best. You may also use canned roasted red peppers, if necessary.

Purée everything together until foamy. Serve immediately with salad.

Geoffrey D. Sandifer, Governor's Mansion Executive Chef

Lowcountry Strawberry Festival at Boone Hall

Mount Pleasant • Spring

The Strawberry Festival at Boone Hall offers four days and nights of fun and festivities. There will be amusement park rides for both large and small attendees as well as pig races, vendor exhibits, games, and concessions. Also offered is a jump pillow, a 3-story slide tower, the spider web, and a rock climbing wall. Special prices are offered for special nights and wrist bands will allow access throughout the 4-day festival. Come join the fun and pick strawberries on your way home.

843.884.4371 • www.boonehallplantation.com

Chicken & Mixed Green Salad with Strawberries

6 cups mixed salad greens
1 cup sliced mixed fresh vegetables (your choice: tomatoes, peppers, cucumber, onion, etc.)
2 cups deboned and chunked grilled chicken
1 cup fresh strawberry slices
Sugared pecans
Goat cheese crumbles
Poppy seed vinaigrette dressing

In a large salad bowl, layer ingredients in order listed.

Rena Keller, Sumter

Geechee Corn Salad in Sweet Vinegar Sauce

Geechee Corn Salad:

3 cups corn, rinsed and well drained
¼ cup chopped green onions
⅓ cup diced red bell peppers
1 cup chopped stewed tomatoes

½ cup minced celery
2 tablespoons sweet onion
Parsley
Salt and pepper to taste

Combine all ingredients in a colander and set aside to drain. If needed, dry vegetables with paper towels to remove as much water as possible. Sprinkle with salt and pepper.

Sweet Vinegar Sauce:

⅓ cup vinegar
⅓ cup sugar
¼ cup oil
½ teaspoon minced garlic

½ teaspoon black pepper
½ teaspoon celery seed
¼ teaspoon red pepper flakes

In a bowl or container with a lid, combine vinegar and sugar, allowing sugar to dissolve. Add remaining ingredients and shake well. Pour over salad and toss several times; chill covered. Toss before serving.

Lowcountry Store

D.C. England/istock/thinkstock

Lowcountry Sweet Potato Salad

3 medium sweet potatoes, cleaned
   and cubed
Salt to taste
⅓ cup dried cranberries
⅓ cup raisins
½ teaspoon cinnamon
½ cup apple cider, divided
½ cup chopped green onions
¼ cup white balsamic vinegar
¼ cup extra virgin olive oil
1½ teaspoons creole seasoning

This is a pretty straightforward recipe for Sweet Potato Salad, which is much like potato salad. You can adjust the amount of some of the ingredients for your own taste. And instead of creole seasoning you can use a store-bought Lowcountry or Gullah seasoning. Season as you like and serve as fresh as possible.

Boil sweet potatoes in salted water until tender but not mushy, about 6 minutes. Drain and refrigerate 6 hours.

In a small saucepan, combine cranberries, raisins, cinnamon and apple cider. Bring to a boil. Reduce heat to a simmer and cook 3 minutes. Strain, reserving the liquid, and refrigerate cranberry mixture. Add enough additional cider to liquid to make ¼ cup. Cover and chill cider.

In a medium mixing bowl, combine chilled sweet potatoes, cranberry mixture, and green onions. In a small mixing bowl, stir together reserved ¼ cup cider liquid, balsamic vinegar, olive oil and creole seasoning. Pour dressing over sweet potato mixture, mix and serve cold.

Sandy Kee, Sumter

Peachy Southern Slaw

Slaw:

1 cup pecan pieces
1 head savoy cabbage, sliced
8 fresh South Carolina peaches, peeled,
    pitted and sliced
1 red bell pepper, sliced
1 yellow bell pepper, sliced
½ cup chopped green onions
2 tablespoons celery seed

We hope your enjoy this version of a traditional Southern slaw that uses the incredible flavor of South Carolina peaches! Combine the mixtures just before serving to keep the flavor fresh and everything crisp. Enjoy!

Place pecan pieces in a skillet and cook over medium heat, stirring constantly, until lightly toasted. In a large bowl, mix toasted pecans, cabbage, sliced peaches, red and yellow bell peppers, green onions and celery seed. Cover and refrigerate 45 minutes.

Dressing:

½ cup chopped fresh South Carolina
    peaches
½ cup vegetable oil
¼ cup honey
¼ cup lemon juice
Salt and pepper to taste

In a blender or food processor, blend chopped peaches until smooth. Transfer to a bowl and mix with oil, honey, lemon juice, salt and pepper. Chill until slaw is ready to be served.

1 bunch fresh mint sprigs for garnish

To serve, toss Slaw with Dressing to coat. Garnish with mint sprigs.

South Carolina Peach Council

Peach Waldorf Salad

6 large South Carolina peaches, peeled,
    pitted and sliced
1 cup diced celery
1 cup chopped walnuts
2 tablespoons honey
½ cup sour cream
Lettuce leaves
Fresh whole strawberries for garnish

This wonderful version of Waldorf Salad adds the flavor of fresh South Carolina peaches. The peaches combined with the walnuts and honey really make for a tasty dish. And, it is very simple to prepare. You may have an instant family favorite!

In a large bowl, toss peaches, celery, walnuts and honey. Chill well. At serving time, fold in sour cream and pile on lettuce leaves on salad plates. Garnish with whole strawberries.

South Carolina Peach Council

AdShooter/istock/thinkstock

Ridge Peach Festival
Trenton • June

Our all-day family festival kicks off with a morning parade led by Fort Gordon Signet military band. The festival features 115 unique arts and crafts, antiques, homemade peach desserts and preserves, peach ice cream, live music all day, rides for the children, a variety of food vendors, and a softball tournament. Shuttles will run all day from the parking area to the park. Come out and enjoy the southern hospitality and richness of this wonderful town. Nestled between Aiken, North Augusta, and Edgefield, SC. This quiet, small town comes alive with the annual Ridge Peach Festival and plays host to more than 15,000 visitors from all across the south.

803.275.9487 • www.ridgepeachfestival.com

Just Eat This
Blue Cheese Apple Slaw

½ cup mayonnaise
1 tablespoon Dijon mustard
¼ cup sugar
3 tablespoons apple cider vinegar
6 large Granny Smith apples, shredded
2 cups shredded red cabbage
1 cup crumbled blue cheese
1 cup chopped, toasted walnuts
Salt to taste

Combine mayonnaise, mustard, sugar and vinegar in a bowl. Add remaining ingredients and lightly toss just to combine.

Chef Chris Casner
Just Eat This, Summerville

This is a great twist on traditional slaw. It goes great with roasted pork and can be made a day ahead.

South Carolina Apple Festival
Westminster • September

Beginning the day after Labor Day and running through the following weekend, the South Carolina Apple Festival celebrates the beginning of apple harvest season in Oconee County, the largest apple-producing area in the state. This fun annual festival has drawn thousands of visitors to Westminster since 1961. Whether you enjoy whitewater rafting, shopping for arts and crafts, browsing antique shops, or just kicking back and listening to live musical entertainment, the Apple Festival offers something for everyone in the family.

864.647.7223 • www.westminstersc.com

Cabbage Salad with Oil Dressing

½ to 1 cup chopped fresh parsley
2 teaspoons sugar or 1 tablespoon
    Splenda
2 tablespoons oil
3 tablespoons white vinegar
1 teaspoon salt

1 large onion, diced
Matchstick carrots (chopped as
    much as you like to make the salad
    colorful)
1 (10-ounce) package Angel Hair Cole
    Slaw

Toss all ingredients until well blended. Refrigerate overnight, stirring periodically and just before serving.

Janet Swope Wade, Aiken

Apple and Orange Fruit Ambrosia

10 medium oranges, peeled and
    separated
1 cup flaked coconut

4 apples, peeled and grated
6 tablespoons powdered sugar

In a large bowl, combine all ingredients and mix well. Chill 3 to 4 hours. Serve as an accompaniment to a meal or as a dessert, if desired.

South Carolina Department of Agriculture

Watermelon, Rosemary and Feta Salad

4 cups chopped watermelon, chilled
2 ounces feta cheese (ideally goat feta), crumbled
1 teaspoon finely chopped fresh rosemary (or dried)
Salt and pepper to taste
High quality olive oil

Toss watermelon, feta and rosemary together; add salt and pepper to taste. You should need very little salt, depending on how salty the feta is. Drizzle a tiny stream of olive oil over everything and toss. Chill until serving. Serves 2 to 4.

Additions: Finely chopped toasted walnuts or finely sliced shallots make a good addition.

Pineapple Pistachio Salad

1 (3.9-ounce) package Jell-O pistachio instant pudding and pie filling
1 (20-ounce) can crushed pineapple in juice, undrained
1 cup mini marshmallows
½ cup chopped pecans
1½ cups whipped topping, thawed

Mix dry pudding mix, pineapple, marshmallows and pecans in large bowl. Add whipped topping; stir gently until well blended. Cover and refrigerate at least 1 hour before serving. Serve on lettuce-covered salad plates garnished with pineapple chunks. Makes 8 (½-cup) servings.

Janice Kara, McColl

Hampton County Watermelon Festival

Hampton • June

Hampton County is the home of the world's original Watermelon Festival. Since 1939, the Hampton County Watermelon Festival has grown to become South Carolina's oldest continuing festival. From the beginning, it has been a celebration of, for, and by the people of this friendly Lowcountry County, timed to the melon harvest every summer. The Watermelon Festival Parade is the longest in the state of South Carolina at 3.2 miles, extending from the Town of Varnville to the Town of Hampton. You will enjoy a Street Dance featuring live music, food, craft and souvenir vendors, fun rides for the kids, and day-long fishing contest. You won't want to miss the Watermelon Eating Contest and the Seed Spitting Contest. And, of course, we will be serving lots of watermelon, watermelon, watermelon. Join us for good family fun!

www.hcmelonfest.org

Watermelon Fruit Boat

1 small oblong watermelon
1 cantaloupe
1 honeydew melon
2 peaches, peeled, cored and cut into bite-size pieces
2 cups strawberry halves
2 cups grape halves
2 kiwifruit, peeled and sliced (optional)

Cut top third lengthwise from watermelon, discard top or use as desired. Scoop balls from larger bottom section of watermelon. Remove seeds; cover balls and refrigerate. Scoop remaining pulp from watermelon with large spoon to form a shell. For decorative edge, cut a scallop or sawtooth design. Drain shell. Cut a thin slice from bottom of shell to flatten it and keep it from tipping over; refrigerate. Halve canteloupe and honeydew, remove seeds and scoop out pulp or cut into bite-size pieces. Refrigerate. When ready to serve, combine fruit in the watermelon shell.

Grandma Lucille's Frosted Cranberry Salad

1 (20-ounce) can crushed pineapple
2 (3-ounce) packages lemon Jell-O mix
7 ounces ginger ale soda
1 (16-ounce) can jellied cranberry sauce
1 (2-ounce) packet Dream Whip topping mix, plus ingredients to prepare per package directions
1 (8-ounce) package cream cheese, softened
1 tablespoon butter
½ cup chopped pecans

One Christmas, my Grandma Lucille decided to ditch the traditional slices of jellied cranberry and introduced us to a frosted cranberry salad. Since learning the recipe, I have introduced it to family and friends on special occasions from Texas to California. Although on first glance it is mistaken as a dessert, we eat this along with the main course, and it is a great compliment to any plate.

Drain pineapple juice into a measuring cup. Add enough water to equal 1 cup. Heat juice in a pan until it begins to boil. Add Jell-O mix and stir until it dissolves. Then, gently stir in ginger ale. Turn off the heat.

In a separate bowl, combine cranberry sauce and crushed pineapple. Pour into a 9x9-inch baking dish. Then pour Jell-O liquid into the dish. Stir until fruit is evenly distributed. Refrigerate until firm.

When cranberry salad is firm, make Dream Whip according to the instructions on the package. Blend softened cream cheese into prepared Dream Whip. Spread topping over salad.

Preheat oven to 350°. Melt butter and pour on pecans. Spread pecans on a baking sheet and bake for 10 minutes. Top salad with buttered pecans to give it a crunch.

Note: To give your recipe a dose of local South Carolina flavor, purchase your pecans from Whitehall Produce in Anderson, South Carolina. You can contact them at (864) 716-2147.

Soccer Player Qiana Martin, Seneca
(www.qianamartin.com)

Vegetables & Other Side Dishes

Dawn's Slow Cooker Macaroni & Cheese, page 105

Belue farms

Any good cook knows that the freshest ingredients lead to the best recipes and results. Since 1955, family-owned Belue Farms has made "fresh" its specialty, providing just-picked produce, grass-fed Angus beef and farm-raised foods from the Upstate region.

In addition to a thriving farm with acres of peaches, berries, melons, vegetables and cattle, Belue Farms operates a store outside the farm's original packing shed. Favorites include Belue Farms Southern specialties like chow-chow, jams and preserves, salsas, pickles and ciders, plus local foods from more than 20 area farmers. You find, raw milk and artisan cheeses, pastured meats and free-range eggs, gluten-free baked goods and local honey—all in one convenient location.

A welcome respite, Belue Farms offer nutritional information about products and farms so customers know their food source. "We like getting to know our customers and helping them explore healthier food choices," explains Harriett Belue. "Understanding where and how food is grown has become vital for a healthy lifestyle. Here, shoppers know they're getting the freshest foods from our farm and others within a 150-mile radius."

Belue Farms also sells gift baskets and wholesome snacks, beverages, hot boiled peanuts, fruit slushies and DeLuxe ice cream. Online, the farm ships seasonal peaches and specialty boxes nationwide. To learn more or to place an order, visit BelueFarms.com.

Belue Farms

Where Local Goodness Grows

3773 Parris Bridge Road
Boiling Springs, SC 29316
864.578.0446 • www.beluefarms.com
Owned and operated by
Mike Belue and Harriett Belue
Open Year Round
Mon-Fri 9 am – 6 pm; Sat 9 am – 5 pm

Lowcountry Fried Corn and Tomatoes

4 to 5 slices bacon
3 (11-ounce) cans whole-kernel corn,
    drained (or fresh corn cut off the cob)
1 (14.5-ounce) can diced tomatoes
    (or 2 cups diced fresh tomato)
1 teaspoon salt
Black pepper to taste
Pinch sugar
¼ cup milk

This easy recipe has many variations. Add all kinds of vegetables for different flavors and colors.

In a skillet, cook bacon and reserve several spoonfuls of drippings in skillet. Drain bacon on paper towels; when cool, crumble. While bacon cools, cook corn in bacon drippings over medium heat. When corn begins to brown, add remaining ingredients, saving milk until last. Stir to mix well and cook off excess moisture.

Mark Walker, Clemson University Football Fan, Clemson

Scalloped Tomatoes

1 medium sweet onion, sliced
Salt and pepper to taste
1 stick (½ cup) butter, divided
1 cup milk
¼ cup all-purpose flour
1 teaspoon salt
3 ripe tomatoes, sliced
1½ cups breadcrumbs

Place sliced onions in a skillet; season with salt and pepper to taste. Add ½ stick butter and cook over medium-low heat until onions are soft (not brown). Layer onions in a glass baking dish. Melt remaining ½ stick butter in small saucepan over medium heat. Add milk and heat. Whip in flour and heat until thick; remove from heat. Whisk in ⅓ cup water if sauce is thick, and 1 teaspoon salt; set aside. Layer tomato slices over onions and cover with white sauce. Top with breadcrumbs and bake at 350° for 40 minutes.

Williams Muscadine Festival
Nesmith • Labor Day Weekend

Bring your tents, campers, and RVs and stay the weekend picking muscadines, enjoying wine tastings, pit-pig barbecue, and fireworks! Tour the vineyard and farm, and learn the history of the early African-American farm. The festival kicks off with a wine tasting on Friday at 7:30 p.m. There will be numerous activities on Saturday 8:00 a.m. to midnight, and on Sunday 1:00 p.m. to midnight. On Monday, the festival winds down but visitors are welcome to socialize and pick muscadines from 8:00 a.m. till dark! There is no admission fee to the festival, and refreshments will be sold.

843.355.7793

Bill's Fried Green Tomatoes

pushenok/istock/thinkstock

1 cup ground cornmeal
1 cup all-purpose flour (not self-rising)
1 tablespoon garlic powder
½ teaspoon cayenne pepper
1½ cups buttermilk
Kosher salt and freshly ground black
    pepper to taste
4 large unripe tomatoes, cut into
    ½-inch thick slices (ends removed)
½ cup vegetable oil
Hot pepper sauce, for serving
Lemon wedges, for serving

In a large bowl, combine cornmeal, flour, garlic powder and cayenne. Pour buttermilk into a separate bowl and season with salt and pepper. Dip tomatoes in buttermilk and dredge in cornmeal mixture, coating both sides well. Place a large cast iron skillet over medium heat and add oil. When oil is hot, pan-fry tomatoes in batches until golden-brown and crispy on both sides, 3 to 4 minutes on each side. Carefully remove tomatoes to paper towels to drain. Serve with hot pepper sauce and lemon wedges.

This recipe also works well with eggplant, sweet onion slices, and even okra.

Bill White, Clemson

Okra with Tomatoes

1½ cups sliced okra
¼ cup chopped onion
½ green bell pepper, chopped
2 tablespoons vegetable oil
1 (14.5-ounce) can tomatoes with juice, or 1½ cups tomato purée

2 teaspoons sugar
1 tablespoon flour blended with 1 tablespoon cold water
½ teaspoon salt
¼ teaspoon pepper

Cook okra in boiling salted water 10 minutes. Drain. In saucepan, brown onion and green bell pepper in oil. Add tomatoes with juice; cook over low heat 5 minutes. Add okra and remaining ingredients. Cook 5 minutes longer.

South Carolina Department of Parks, Recreation & Tourism

Charleston Okra Pilau

4 slices bacon, chopped
1 onion, chopped
1 tablespoon minced green bell pepper

2 cups stewed tomatoes
2 cups thinly sliced okra
Salt and black pepper to taste
2 cups rice

Fry bacon in a deep skillet. Remove bacon, reserving drippings. Sauté onion and bell pepper in drippings until onions are golden brown. Add tomatoes and okra and cook over medium heat, stirring occasionally, while preparing rice. Season with salt and pepper.

In a large saucepan, combine 2 quarts water, 1 teaspoon salt and rice. Bring to a boil, then boil 12 minutes; drain well. In the top of a double-boiler, combine drained rice with tomato mixture. Bring water in bottom of double-boiler to a light boil and cook pilau 15 to 20 minutes. Add bacon just before serving. Makes 6 servings.

Black Pepper and Onion Fried Okra

1 pound fresh okra
½ cup self-rising flour
1 cup self-rising cornmeal
¼ to ⅓ cup finely chopped onion
½ tablespoon black pepper
Dash salt
1 cup vegetable oil for frying

Wash okra in cold water, making sure any dirt is removed. Cut off tops and stems; slice. Don't rinse because inner juices help keep the breading on. In a large bowl, mix flour, cornmeal, onion, pepper and salt. Add okra. Mix to evenly coat, let sit 5 minutes; mix again. In frying pan, cook okra in oil until golden brown on all sides. Drain on paper towels. Serve hot.

Miss B., Beaufort

Fresh okra is best if you can get some in season. If not, the store-bought sliced frozen type will do. Just let it thaw real good before cooking.

Margaret Edwards/istock/thinkstock

Rice & Butter Beans

1 (1-pound) package large lima beans
6 to 8 cups water
3 tablespoons oil
1 medium onion, chopped
1 green scallion, chopped
½ cup finely chopped celery
½ green bell pepper, chopped
½ tablespoon minced garlic
1½ pounds smoked sausage, sliced
1 tablespoon Worcestershire sauce
2 teaspoons soy sauce
2 tablespoons salt
1 tablespoon ground white pepper
2 tablespoons Cajun seasoning
1 teaspoon onion powder

In a large stockpot, cook beans in water. Bring to a boil, then reduce heat and simmer about 2 hours, covered. Sauté vegetables in oil with garlic, and sausage. About an hour before beans are done, add vegetables and sausage and remaining ingredients. Cook until beans are done. Add a bit of cornstarch or flour to thicken, or milk or water to thin, if needed. Adjust spices to taste and serve over cooked rice in a bowl with hot sauce on the side and a cornbread muffin.

Bill White, Clemson

Saint Stephen Catfish Festival
Saint Stephen • 1st Weekend in April

The Saint Stephen Catfish Festival is a fun hometown festival featuring rides, live bands, clowns, a Catfish Stew Cook-Off, Sweet-Pea Contest, and all types of food, plus craft and commercial vendors. The Catfish Festival is FREE to the public. Come and try our award-winning Catfish Stews and spend the day enjoying some good family fun at the Catfish Festival in St. Stephen, South Carolina.

843.567.3597

Black & White Beans with Onions & Peppers

2 tablespoons olive oil or vegetable oil
1 cup finely chopped red onion
2 cloves garlic, minced
⅓ cup red wine vinegar
¼ cup chopped green bell pepper
¼ cup chopped red bell pepper
2 tablespoons minced parsley
2 tablespoons sugar
¼ teaspoon salt
¼ teaspoon pepper
1 (16-ounce) can great Northern beans, rinsed and drained
1 (16-ounce) can black beans, rinsed and drained
Red and green bell pepper rings for garnish

Heat oil in medium skillet, sauté onions and garlic until crisp-tender. Remove from heat and cool. Stir in vinegar, chopped green and red bell peppers, parsley, sugar, salt and pepper. Combine beans in serving bowl, pour onion mixture over top; mix well. Garnish with bell pepper rings.

Karen Burns, Charleston

Kingstree / Bi-Lo Pig Pickin'

Kingstree • October

Each autumn, the Town of Kingstree hosts a hometown festival that brings folks from everywhere. What exactly is "Pig Pickin' "? It's the best way to eat hot-off-the-fire barbeque. Whether you call it pullin', pickin' or just plain eatin', you're sure to come around to our way of thinkin' when you taste that first juicy strip of vinegar-sauce riddled pork melting in your mouth. Hear crowds as they check out the competitions, purchase craft or baked items, and see smiling faces of folks enjoying the good life.

843.355.7484

Big Jim's Chili Beans

2 (15½-ounce) cans light red
   kidney beans
2 (15½-ounce) cans dark red kidney
   beans
2 (14½-ounce) cans diced tomatoes
1 (16-ounce) jar salsa
4 teaspoons chili powder, or to taste
2 pounds lean hamburger meat
1 medium onion, diced

Mix beans, tomatoes, salsa and chili powder in large slow cooker set on high. Brown meat and onion in pan; add to slow cooker. Cook 3 hours on medium, stirring frequently. Set to lowest setting until ready to serve. Serve with sliced sharp cheese, sweet pickles and crackers or hushpuppies. Serves 4 to 7.

Big Jim Meaders, Mauldin

This is my tried-and-true chili bean recipe, I make it every couple of months. It's one of my family favorites for Super Bowl games, pot luck dinners, etc. I've been cooking for years and have been asked for this recipe many times. Guests always want to take home the leftovers.

Hoppin' John

1 cup chopped onion
1 tablespoon bacon drippings
2 (16-ounce) cans black-eyed peas,
    slightly drained, or about 3 cups
    cooked black-eyed peas

1 cup chopped cooked ham
¼ teaspoon ground cayenne pepper
3 cups hot cooked rice
Salt to taste
Sliced sweet onion (optional)

In a large saucepan, sauté onion in bacon drippings until tender. Stir in black-eyed peas, ham and cayenne pepper; simmer 10 minutes. Stir in hot cooked rice and salt. Serve Hoppin' John hot with sliced onion and cornbread.

Traditional Preparation of Hoppin' John

Tradition says that eating Hoppin' John, collard greens and cornbread on New Year's Day will bring a year filled with good luck. Made of black-eyed peas and rice, seasoned with ham hocks, onions, green peppers, and spices, the origin of the name is unknown, but it's thought to be a slave dish from the colonial era. *New Southern Cooking* author Natalie Dupree said that the black-eyed peas are said to represent each Confederate soldier who died for the South during the Civil War.

South Carolina Department of Parks, Recreation & Tourism

Lowcountry Meat 'n Collards

¼ cup olive oil
2 tablespoons minced garlic
5 cups chicken stock
1 smoked turkey drumstick, ham or pork fatback
5 bunches collard greens, rinsed, trimmed and chopped
Salt and black pepper to taste
1 tablespoon crushed red pepper flakes (optional)
Hot sauce to taste (optional)

Heat olive oil in a large pot over medium heat. Add garlic and gently cook until light brown. Pour in chicken stock and add turkey leg or pork. Cover pot and simmer 20 to 30 minutes. Add collard greens and turn the heat up to medium-high. Let the greens cook down for about 45 minutes, gently stirring about every 10 minutes. After 45 minutes, reduce heat to medium and season lightly with salt and pepper. Continue to cook 50 minutes to 1 hour until greens are tender and dark. Drain before serving. Reserve some liquid in case you have leftovers so you can reheat in the liquid. Season with red pepper flakes and hot sauce, as desired.

Note: You can use ham, pork fatback or even smoked turkey for your meat seasoning.

Collard and Barbecue Festival
Gaston • 1st Weekend in October

Celebrate fall harvest at the annual Gaston Collard Festival with a parade, rides, games, and live entertainment. There's even a beauty pageant, but the real queen of the festival is the collard. And, of course, more fixin's like rice and cornbread will be available. You will enjoy our live auction, craft vendors, chili cook-off, and dessert contest. But best of all is our famous collards, so join us for some good family fun. 131 North Carlisle Street in Gaston.

803.796.7725 • gastonsc.org

Home Team BBQ Collards

1 gallon water
3 cups cider vinegar
¼ cup hot sauce
½ cup brown sugar
¼ cup kosher salt
2 to 3 shoulder bones or smoked ham hocks
2 pound collard greens, cut into 2-inch strips
½ pound smoked pork shoulder, chopped or
   pulled

*Collards done right!
I started Fiery Ron's Home Team
BBQ in the style of an old Mississippi
juke joint right here in South
Carolina. Originally from Atlanta,
then moving to New York, then Aspen,
Colorado, and then back to the South
to South Carolina, I combined my
culinary education, knowledge, and
experience into a unique Southern
fare. This is a hometown recipe that is
full of flavor.*

Bring water to a simmer in large stockpot. Add cider vinegar, hot sauce, brown sugar and salt. Add bones or ham hocks for flavor, and simmer 25 minutes. Add collard greens and smoked pork. Simmer lightly for 2 to 3 hours or until tender.

Aaron Siegel, Fiery Ron's Home Team BBQ, Sullivan's Island

Kent Whitaker

Harvard Beets

½ cup sugar
2 teaspoons cornstarch
½ cup vinegar

2 tablespoons butter
1 (16-ounce) can beets, drained

Mix sugar, cornstarch and vinegar in saucepan. Stir over low heat until thickened. Add butter and beets; stir well. Remove from heat and allow to rest 30 minutes. If not warm enough, heat before serving. Yields 4 servings.

Janice Karas, McColl

Lowcountry Taters and Green Beans

3 cups thinly sliced potatoes
2 cups frozen green beans
½ teaspoon dried thyme
¼ teaspoon ground black pepper
1 teaspoon vegetarian Worcestershire sauce
1 cup vegetable broth, divided
1 teaspoon cornstarch
¼ cup chopped fresh parsley

You can call this Lowcountry or sometimes we jokingly call it Low Economy! Either way here is a very easy recipe for potatoes and beans.

In a large skillet over medium-high heat, combine potatoes, green beans, thyme, pepper, Worcestershire sauce and ¾ cup broth. Bring to a boil. Reduce heat to medium-low, cover and simmer 15 to 20 minutes or until vegetables are tender. In a small bowl, blend remaining ¼ cup broth and cornstarch. Stir in parsley; add to potato mixture. Cook, stirring, until bubbly and thickened.

Sandy Kee, Sumter

Glazed Carrots

15 small carrots
6 tablespoons butter or margarine
½ lemon, juiced
3 tablespoons brown sugar

Scrape carrots and cut in half length-wise. Boil in salted water until tender, drain well. Melt butter or margarine in a heavy skillet. Add lemon juice and brown sugar; heat, stirring until mixture becomes thick. Add carrots and heat, spooning syrup over them until well glazed.

Janice Kara, McColl

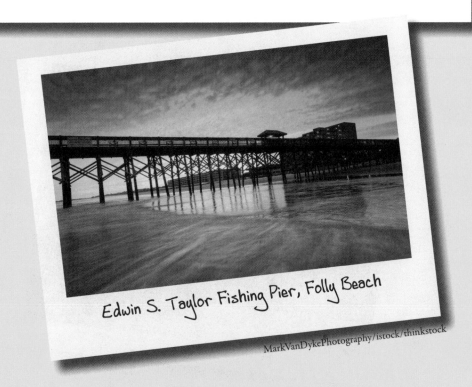

Edwin S. Taylor Fishing Pier, Folly Beach

MarkVanDykePhotography/istock/thinkstock

Mimi Flenniken's Special Scalloped Potatoes

2 to 3 pounds potatoes
1 (10¾-ounce) can cream of chicken soup
½ cup sour cream
¼ cup mayonnaise

Salt and pepper to taste
¾ medium sweet onion, sliced
1 cup cubed ham
¾ cup grated Cheddar cheese
2 tablespoon soft butter, divided

Peel potatoes and parboil in water to cover; slice when cool. Combine soup, sour cream, mayonnaise, salt and pepper. In a 9x13-inch baking dish, layer ½ potatoes, ½ onion slices, ½ ham, ½ soup mixture, ½ cheese and 1 tablespoon butter; repeat. Bake at 350° for 30 to 40 minutes until onions are cooked.

Lynn Harper in honor of Mimi Flenniken, Darlington

Laura Clay-Ballard/istock/thinkstock

Karen's Heavenly Creamy Mashed Potatoes

3½ pounds russet potatoes, peeled, 1-inch cubed
1 (8-ounce) package cream cheese, softened
½ cup sour cream
½ cup whole milk
¾ cup chopped fresh chives (about 3 bunches)
1 tablespoon creamed horseradish
¼ teaspoon salt
½ teaspoon white pepper
1 tablespoon chilled butter, cut into small pieces
½ cup grated Parmesan cheese

The key to this recipe is the softened cream cheese and the horseradish. The cream cheese mixes so well with the potatoes when it's not cold and stiff. And the horseradish adds extra zing to the flavor. This recipe is different from normal mashed potatoes and has become a favorite family of my family.

Grease a 9x13-inch glass baking dish. Boil potatoes in water to cover with a pinch of salt until tender, about 15 minutes. Drain potatoes and mash with cream cheese. Make sure cream cheese is soft so that you don't over work the potatoes. Add sour cream, milk, chives, horseradish, salt and pepper. Spoon into greased baking dish and dot with butter. Sprinkle with Parmesan cheese. Bake at 350° until browned on top. Top with your favorite shredded cheese and even bacon bits, if desired. Serve hot.

Karen Burns, Charleston

Gullah Potato Bake

1 sweet potato (about 8 ounces),
   peeled
6 to 8 potatoes, peeled
1 onion
¼ cup olive oil

1 cup cream
4 eggs
1 cup shredded Swiss cheese
1 teaspoon sugar
Dash salt

Preheat oven to 350°. Thinly slice sweet potato, potatoes and onion. Sauté in olive oil until golden brown. Layer in a greased half-sheet baking pan. Beat cream with eggs; stir in shredded Swiss cheese, sugar and salt; pour over potatoes. Bake 30 to 40 minutes, until firm.

Georgetown Light, North Island

Andrew F. Kazmierski/istock/thinkstock

Sweet Potato & Apple Bake

2 pounds fresh South Carolina sweet potatoes
1½ pounds South Carolina cooking apples
Fruit juice
⅔ cup light brown sugar
6 tablespoons margarine
3 tablespoons maple syrup
½ cup apple cider
1 tablespoon lemon juice
1 teaspoon cinnamon
½ teaspoon ground ginger

Sweet potatoes are a South Carolina and Southern favorite. Sweet potatoes can be grown across the state but do best in sandy soil. In South Carolina there are about eight main varieties of sweet potatoes commonly grown. This recipe works well no matter what part of the state your sweet potatoes came from or what type they are. And when selecting apples, don't forget—apples from South Carolina are the perfect choice.

Boil sweet potatoes; cool, skin and slice ¼-inch thick. Peel apples; quarter, core and slice ¼-inch thick. Place apples in fruit juice to cover to prevent discoloration; set aside. In small saucepan, bring sugar, margarine, cider, syrup, lemon juice, cinnamon and ginger to a boil. Reduce heat and cook 10 minutes, stirring constantly. Drain apples well and pat dry. Arrange apples and sweet potatoes in a 9x13-inch baking dish. Cover with sauce. Bake 25 to 30 minutes at 325°, basting occasionally.

South Carolina Department of Agriculture

Sausage and Giblet Dirty Rice

1 cup uncooked white rice
2½ cups chicken broth, divided
6 ounces chicken giblets
6 ounces chicken livers
6 ounces ground pork sausage
½ stick butter
¾ cup finely chopped onion
¼ cup finely chopped celery
2 cloves garlic, chopped
½ teaspoon ground black pepper
½ teaspoon white pepper
1 teaspoon cayenne pepper

Cook rice in 2 cups chicken broth. While rice cooks, chop or grind giblets and liver. Stir in ground pork sausage, and place in a large frying pan with a cover. Fry meat mixture in butter until no longer pink. Stir and break apart any large clumps until only small pieces remain. Add onion, celery, garlic and peppers. Fry or sauté about 5 minutes. Add remaining ½ cup chicken stock and cooked rice; combine well. Cover and simmer over low heat 8 to 10 minutes until heated through or until liquid is reduced.

Kelly Brown
for her dad Bill and his wife Jean
of Ninety Six

Colleton County Rice Festival
Walterboro • April

The Colleton County Rice Festival is a celebration of the rice-planting heritage that helped found Colleton County. The fun-filled family festival features parades, petting zoo and face painting for the kids, street dances, blue grass/gospel/country and pop entertainers, food and arts 'n' crafts vendors, a golf tournament, 5K run, dog shows, rice-cooking contests, horseshoe tournament, and fireworks display. Come see why Walterboro is the front porch of the Lowcountry and enjoy three fun-filled days of family activities in the warm Carolina sun.

843.549.1079 • www.ricefestival.org

South Carolina Red Rice with Ham and Bacon

8 strips thick bacon
1 large onion, chopped (sweet if desired)
3 green onions (scallions), bulb and green stem, minced
2 ripe plum tomatoes, peeled, seeded and chopped
¾ cup minced or finely chopped cooked ham
1 cup uncooked white rice
Salt to taste
Hot sauce to taste

Preheat oven to 350°. In a heavy skillet or cast iron pan over medium-high heat, cook bacon strips until crisp. Remove bacon and drain on paper towels. Leave about ½ remaining bacon fat in the pan, and reserve the rest. Sauté onion and green onions in the bacon fat until edges are browned. Crumble bacon and add back into the skillet. Add tomatoes, ham, rice, salt and hot sauce. Reduce by cooking over low heat for 10 minutes. If needed, add a spoonful of bacon grease. Remove from heat. Spoon the mixture into greased 2-quart casserole dish. Cover with foil and bake 1 hour, stirring occasionally. Remove foil for the last 10 to 15 minutes of cooking. Serve hot with greens, cornbread and hot sauce.

Note: Any type or cut of ham will do— thin cut country ham, leftover ham, chopped ham, etc.

Kelly Brown
for her dad Bill and his wife Jean of Ninety Six

Coastal Carolina Lowcountry Red Rice

4 slices bacon
1 small sweet or yellow onion, chopped
1 cup long-grain white rice
1 (14.5-ounce) can diced or crushed
   tomatoes
1 teaspoon salt
1 teaspoon black pepper
½ teaspoon garlic powder
Hot sauce or cayenne pepper to taste
1 cup chicken stock
¼ cup water

This recipe from my mother's family near Charleston. She served rice at every meal. She could make just about anything good with all kinds of seasoned rice. This goes great with cornbread and greens. And it is really good with chicken and seafood. She called it Lowcountry rice, or Gullah rice. Depends on who she was talking to, I guess. We just called it Mom's cooking. I didn't know we were eating Lowcountry and Gullah food. It was just dinner like everybody else had.

Cook bacon in a covered pot or skillet. Drain on a paper towel; crumble and cool. Reserve ½ drippings leaving ½ in skillet. Add onions and cook until tender. Add rice and brown the edges. Add a spoonful of reserved bacon drippings, if needed. Add remaining ingredients, except bacon. Stir to mix and bring to a boil. Boil 1 to 2 minutes; reduce heat and cover. Cook as you would normally cook rice, about 30 minutes. Don't lift the lid. Serve hot topped with crumbled bacon, or stir in bacon just before serving.

Darnel Brantley, Clemson

Dawn's Slow Cooker Macaroni & Cheese

16 ounces macaroni
2 (12-ounce) cans evaporated milk
3 cups milk
4 cups shredded sharp Cheddar cheese
2 cups shredded medium Cheddar cheese
½ cup melted margarine
4 eggs
Salt and pepper

This is a really tasty macaroni and cheese recipe cooked in a slow cooker. It's almost too easy! People ask me for the recipe all of the time. It's a standard at family events.

Boil macaroni until cooked; drain. Combine with remaining ingredients in a slow cooker and stir to mix. Cover and cook on low for 3½ hours.

Dawn Gleuck Brit, Columbia

Historic Middleton Place, Dorchester County,

Alexander Fox/istock/thinkstock

Grandma's Mac and Cheese

1½ cups uncooked macaroni
2 tablespoons butter
2 tablespoons flour
1 teaspoon dry mustard
1 teaspoon salt
¼ teaspoon pepper

2 cups milk
8 ounces sharp Cheddar cheese, cubed
¾ cup crumbs of any kind
    (breadcrumbs, cracker crumbs,
    panko, etc.)

Preheat oven to 400°. Cook macaroni as directed on package; drain. In medium saucepan, melt butter over low heat. Add flour, dry mustard, salt and pepper, and stir quickly until well mixed. Add milk and blend well with wire whip. Add cheese; stir until melted and sauce is thick and smooth. Put cooked macaroni in 3-quart casserole dish and add cheese sauce. Sprinkle crumbs over top and bake about 30 minutes or until it starts to bubble.

Amy Miller, Charleston
The Navy Wives of South Carolina Recipes

South Carolina porch waiting for a good conversation.

Leslie Haywood

Miss B's Easy Vegetable Cornbread Casserole

A QUICK NOTE: You need to plan ahead for this casserole because the mix must be refrigerated at least 4 hours or overnight for best results.

1 (8-ounce) box cornbread stuffing mix
2 cups frozen mixed vegetables, slightly
   thawed
1½ cups cubed cooked ham
1 cup shredded Cheddar cheese, divided
3 eggs, beaten
2 cups milk
Salt and pepper to taste

This is an easy variation of a casserole that I grew up with. Many times people made this from leftover hardened cornbread and leftover vegetables. That way you didn't have much waste. You really don't need too much seasoning if your cornbread stuffing already has it. But you can add some extra spices if you want to try something different.

Spray an 8x12-inch glass baking dish with nonstick cooking spray, or grease with butter. In the baking dish, combine dry stuffing mix, vegetables, ham and ½ cup cheese. In a bowl, mix together eggs, milk, salt and pepper until well blended. Gently pour egg mixture over dry cornbread mixture. Don't stir or mix. Spread with a spoon to evenly coat. Cover and refrigerate at least 4 hours or overnight. Preheat oven to 350°. Remove cover and bake 20 to 30 minutes until almost done. Top with remaining ½ cup cheese, and bake an additional 5 to 10 minutes until cheese is melted and golden brown. You may need to adjust cooking time depending on your oven and how long you let the mix rest. A knife inserted in middle should come out very clean.

Miss B., Beaufort

Double Crust Tomato, Onion and Bacon Pie

4 very ripe tomatoes
Salt and pepper to taste
½ medium onion
¾ cup shredded Cheddar cheese
¾ cup shredded Monterey Jack cheese
3 slices bacon, cooked and crumbled
3 tablespoons mayonnaise (use real
   mayo or it'll be watery)
1 (9-inch) double pie crust
1 teaspoon dried basil, divided

Two years ago I stumbled upon the deliciousness that is tomato pie and I used it in my Home-ec 101 cooking blog. The origin of this recipe can be credited to Paula Dean, but it has undergone many tweaks. If you need to, you can cheat a bit and use a store bought refrigerated pie crust if you are in a hurry. And, I suggest that you use real mayo or it'll be watery. And, you can even use cream cheese in place of mayonnaise. I hope you enjoy the recipe.

Preheat oven to 425°. Core each tomato, removing the hard area around the stem. Cut in half through the equator. Use your finger to scoop out the seeds; discard seeds. Slice. Place sliced tomatoes in a colander over a large bowl or the sink and sprinkle with salt and pepper. Allow tomatoes to sit while preparing the other ingredients. Slice onion very thinly...no, a bit thinner. Not yet, a little thinner still. In a bowl, combine cheeses, bacon and mayonnaise. Mix thoroughly. Carefully lay 1 pie crust in a 9-inch pie plate. Arrange a layer of ½ tomato slices, ½ onion slices and ½ teaspoon dried basil. Repeat with remaining tomatoes, onion and basil. Top with cheese mixture. Top with second crust, seal edges, and cut slits in the top. Use water to glue on any decorative touches. Bake 45 minutes, checking after 30. Place foil on edges to protect from burning. Allow to cool at least 10 minutes on wire rack. If you can wait longer to slice the pie, the cheese won't be as runny... but I LIKE the cheese to be runny. Enjoy.

Heather Solos, Moncks Corner
www.home-ec101.com

Easy Onion & Cheese Pie

1 (9-inch) pie crust
¼ cup Italian dressing
2 tablespoons butter
2 large onions, chopped
1 cup shredded Cheddar cheese
2 to 3 eggs

½ cup heavy cream
2 teaspoons ground sage
1 teaspoon crushed dried marjoram
   leaves
½ teaspoon black pepper

Preheat oven to 400°. Pierce bottom of pie crust with fork. Bake 8 minutes or until lightly brown. Cool pie crust completely. In large pan, heat Italian dressing and butter over medium heat; add onions and cook until tender. Fill cooled pie crust with cheese and pour in onion mixture. In a bowl beat eggs, cream, sage, marjoram and pepper; pour over onions. Bake 35 minutes or until golden brown.

Kelly Brown
for her dad Bill and his wife Jean of Ninety Six

James Clarke/istock/thinkstock

Randy's Pear Relish

10 to 15 medium pears, not too ripe
3 green bell peppers
3 red bell peppers
3 yellow bell peppers
1 to 2 onions
1 (4-ounce) jar diced pimentos
4 cups sugar
4 to 5 cups white vinegar
2 tablespoons pickling spice in a tea bag
Dash salt and turmeric

This relish recipe is for canning. I make it with pears from the tree in my back yard. We have an apple, a peach, and a pear tree. The only one that has produced is the pear, and they get big—almost the size of a softball. I had one that I think weighed about FIVE pounds!

Wash, peel, seed and quarter pears. Finely chop pears, bell peppers, onions and pimentos in a food processor. Add to a large saucepan (including juice) with remaining ingredients. Simmer over medium heat about 4 hours or until very tender. Remove spice bag and can in glass jars.

Variation: Make this spicy by adding seeded chopped jalapeño peppers while cooking.

Randy Tumblin, Laurens

Beef & Pork

Randy's Dual Meat
Barbecue, page 138

Chattooga Belle Farm is a 138-acre working farm and event barn located in the shadows of the majestic Blue Ridge Mountains in the western corner of South Carolina. After years of neglect, the orchards were overtaken and the legacy lay hidden until someone saw what once was and what could be. Thousands of new trees plus vineyards and berry patches were planted welcoming the public to enjoy this special place.

There is something for everyone on the farm. Family-friendly activities include various U-pick fruit trees including apples, peaches, and plums plus raspberry and blueberry patches. The charming farm store offers just picked produce, regional food specialties, grass fed farm beef and unique merchandise. The first Sunday of every October, the farm hosts a farm-to-table dinner in the vineyard featuring all local foods prepared by award-winning local chefs.

While visiting the farm, guests will experience the extraordinary flavors of wines made with grapes and other fruits grown in the vineyard and orchards, offering over eight different varieties including the regional Southern specialty Muscadine and Scuppernong Wine.

After working up an appetite from walking the grounds or just enjoying the peaceful mountain breeze, Belle's Bistro is the perfect place to unwind with lunch featuring many delicious items straight from the farm. After lunch, visitors may enjoy a game on the 18-hole disc golf course or just relax in a rocking chair and take in the sweeping mountain views.

The event barn is the ideal location for weddings, family reunions, and corporate retreats or any special occasion that calls for a setting like no other. The barn offers spectacular views of three states with 7,000 flexible square feet of space including a heated inside great room, covered patio area and lawn space for tents.

Conveniently located close to large metro areas including Atlanta, Greenville and Asheville, visiting the farm is an easy day trip. Chattooga Belle Farm... unlike any place on Earth.

Chattooga Belle Farm

454 Damascus Church Road
Long Creek, SC 29658
864-647-9768
www.chattoogabellefarm.com

Beef Spare Ribs with BBQ Sauce

5 pounds beef spareribs
1 cup sugar
½ medium yellow onion, diced
1 tablespoon molasses
¼ cup Worcestershire sauce
⅓ cup soy sauce
¼ cup cider vinegar
¼ cup chili sauce
1 (6-ounce) can tomato paste
1 tablespoon prepared mild yellow mustard
3 cloves garlic, peeled and crushed
1 teaspoon prepared horseradish
Fresh ground pepper to taste

kivoart/istock/thinkstock

Preheat oven to 350°. Cut ribs into serving size portions. (They will be way too messy to do it later.) Use a blender or food processor to combine remaining ingredients. Slather ribs with sauce (you won't use it all) and place fatty-side-up in a shallow roasting pan. Cover and bake 45 minutes. Drain drippings. Baste with additional sauce. Uncover and continue to bake 75 to 90 minutes longer, turning and basting with additional sauce halfway through. Enjoy!

Heather Solos, Moncks Corner
www.home-ec101.com

Though this recipe has a lengthy cook time, there is little prep or monitoring required, so I recommend it for a lazy day.

Tenderloin Steaks with Spinach-Almond Pesto and Brown Rice

Spinach-Almond Pesto:

2 cups fresh baby spinach
2 tablespoons toasted sliced almonds
2 tablespoons shredded Parmesan cheese
1 clove garlic, coarsely chopped
2 tablespoons water
1 tablespoon olive oil
Salt to taste

Hope you enjoy this great recipe. The pesto and rice really complement the flavor of South Carolina beef tenderloin steaks.

Place spinach, toasted almonds, cheese and garlic in food processor. Cover and process until coarse paste forms. With motor running, slowly add water and oil until smooth. Season with salt; set aside.

Steak:

2 (5- to 6-ounce) beef tenderloin steaks, cut 1½-inches thick

Preheat oven to 350°. Heat oven-proof, nonstick skillet over medium heat. Place steaks in skillet and brown 2 minutes. Turn steaks over and place skillet into preheated oven; cook 13 to 18 minutes for medium-rare to medium doneness, turning once. Remove steaks from oven when internal temperature reaches 135° for medium-rare; 150° for medium doneness. Remove steaks from pan; tent loosely with aluminum foil. Let stand 5 to 10 minutes. Temperature will continue to rise about 10° to reach 145° for medium-rare; 160° for medium doneness.

Brown Rice:

½ cup uncooked whole grain brown rice
1 cup water
½ teaspoon salt (optional)
1 cup fresh baby spinach
1 tablespoon minced garlic
2 tablespoons chopped dried cherries
Sliced almonds for garnish

While meat cooks, prepare rice with water and salt according to package directions. Chop spinach. During last 5 minutes of cooking, add chopped spinach and garlic to rice, and continue to cook. When done, remove from heat, add cherries and 1 tablespoon Spinach Almond Pesto to rice; stir to combine.

Serve steaks over rice with remaining pesto. Garnish rice with sliced almonds, if desired.

Roy Copelan, South Carolina Beef Board, Columbia

Meat in the Creek Sirloin

4 sirloin steaks, cut ½-inch thick
Oil or butter for steak
Salt and pepper to taste
1 stick (½ cup) butter, divided
1 medium red onion, diced
4 ounces sliced mushrooms (white or cremini)
1 pint Up the Creek beer (IPA or IIPA)
1 teaspoon thyme
1 teaspoon chopped curled leaf parsley
1 teaspoon marjoram or oregano
¼ teaspoon nutmeg
2 tablespoons all-purpose flour

Up The Creek is our Red Mahogany beer made with a low temp method that increases the fermented sugars but keeps sweetness down. The color and flavor of Up The Creek combined with the cast iron skillet make for a great Meat in the Creek Sirloin recipe. Oh, for those that don't know IPA stands for India Pale Ale. Enjoy—and I'll see ya Up The Creek!

Preheat grill to medium-high heat (approximately 350° to 400°). Allow steaks to reach room temperature; rub steaks with small amount of oil or butter and season on both sides with salt and pepper. Place steaks on grill and brown both sides, 1 to 2 minutes per side. Next, place a cast iron skillet over medium-heat and add ½ stick butter, onion, mushrooms and ½ teaspoon salt. Allow to sweat until onions become translucent and vegetables have surrendered the majority of their liquid. Add beer, thyme, parsley, marjoram and nutmeg to vegetables in skillet; combine until liquid base is formed. Place steaks into skillet with liquid and reduce heat to low. Allow to stew until tender. Sauce should be able to coat the back of a spoon. To thicken, alternate remaining ½ stick butter and flour near the end of cooking, beginning and ending with butter. Make sure all butter has melted and all flour has been absorbed before making any more additions. Sauce will thicken as it cools.

Christopher McElveen, Thomas Creek Brewery, Greenville

London Broil

⅓ cup fresh orange juice
¼ cup minced fresh rosemary
¼ cup olive oil
3 garlic cloves, minced
1 teaspoon salt
1 teaspoon ground black pepper
1 (2-pound) London Broil (top round)

In a large resealable plastic bag, combine orange juice, rosemary, olive oil, garlic, salt, and pepper. Add London broil; seal bag, and refrigerate at least 4 hours or up to 24 hours.

Spray grill rack with nonstick cooking spray, and preheat grill to medium-high heat (350° to 400°). Remove meat from bag, discarding marinade. Grill 7 to 8 minutes per side (keep grill lid closed) or until a thermometer inserted in thickest portion registers 135°. Rest meat 10 minutes before slicing across the grain.

Jack Puccio/istock/thinkstock

Not Yo Mama's Pimento Cheese "Sandwich"

Marinade:

⅓ cup olive oil
1 teaspoon salt
1 tablespoon garlic
1 teaspoon Worcestershire sauce
1 teaspoon Dijon mustard

Combine all ingredients in zip-close bag.

4 (8-ounce) fillets, each 2-inches thick

Cut fillets across the middle lengthwise to make 8 (1-inch) fillets. Keep the 2 "halves" together—this is the "bread" of the sandwich. Add steaks to Marinade; refrigerate 3 to 6 hours. About 30 minutes prior to grilling, bring steaks up to room temperature.

Pimento Cheese:

2 cups shredded Cheddar cheese, room temperature
1 (4-ounce) jar chopped pimentos

½ cup mayonnaise
Dash Worcestershire sauce
Salt and pepper to taste

Mix all Pimento Cheese ingredients while meat comes up to room temperature and set aside.

Keep track of each person's preference for steak temperatures. This is where Grill Charms come in handy. Sear fillets on the grill 1 minute per side, then lower temperature or use indirect heat for 3 more minutes per side for rare, 3½ minutes for medium-rare, 4 per side for medium, 5 per side for medium-well. (If you cook a fillet any more than medium-well, then...well...YOU figure it out, because I have no idea!) Every grill and cut of meat is different, so check and adjust accordingly. When steaks are ready, remove from grill and allow them to rest 5 minutes.

To serve, place 1 fillet "half" on a plate, spread with Pimento Cheese, then top with the other half. Add a pat of butter on top for good measure! Makes 4 servings.

Leslie Haywood, Charleston
Inventor and founder of Grill Charms • www.grillcharms.com

> *In Charleston, grilling is a year-round sport. Grilling for a Lowcountry crowd is one reason I invented the grilling gadget Grill Charms. It's tough to keep track of who wants want on the grill while enjoying a bit of "the beverages," watching the sunset over the marsh, chatting with friends, AND making sure the children don't fall off the dock into the pluff mud. As a red-blooded, all-American, carnivorous Carolina Girl, I want to share a new "beefy" take on the southern staple, the pimento cheese sandwich. And I use the word "sandwich" loosely. Not a stitch of bread in this baby!!*

Tidwell's Tailgate Pimento Cheese Burger

Pimento Cheese:

3 ounces jarred diced pimentos, drained
3 ounces cream cheese, softened
1½ cups shredded sharp Cheddar cheese
1½ cups shredded Pepper Jack cheese
3 tablespoons mayonnaise

Combine ingredients in a bowl; cover and chill before serving. To make it easier to serve on the go, form into small patties the size of each burger; place on wax paper and chill or freeze before heading to the game. Since you never really know how much each person will want, I leave it in a bowl.

Burgers:

2 pounds ground beef (I use ground chuck)
1 tablespoon minced garlic
2 tablespoons minced onion

3 tablespoons steak sauce
1 to 2 tablespoons yellow mustard
Salt and pepper to taste
Buns of your choice

Mix burger ingredients together and form into 6 to 8 patties or 12 mini slider burgers. For a different flavor, substitute beer or wine for the steak sauce. Cook over medium-high heat to desired doneness. Serve on buns topped with Pimento Cheese.

Gerald Tidwell, Proud Gamecock Father, Columbia

Meatballs & Gravy

½ pound ground beef (or 1 pound if
  you don't want to use pork)
½ pound ground pork
½ green bell pepper, finely chopped
2 tablespoons minced onion
1 egg, beaten

1 (5-ounce) can evaporated milk
1 teaspoon salt
¼ teaspoon pepper
½ cup fine breadcrumbs
½ cup flour
½ cup oil for frying

In a large bowl, combine meat, peppers, onions, egg, milk, salt, pepper and breadcrumbs. Mix well using your hands. Roll into ½-inch balls; roll in flour. Heat oil in a shallow skillet over medium-high heat. Brown meatballs, working in batches, turning to brown on all sides. Remove to paper towels to drain. Pour all but 2 tablespoons drippings from skillet; use same skillet to make gravy.

Meatball Gravy:

2 tablespoons flour
1 cup evaporated milk

1 cup water
Salt and pepper to taste

Over medium heat, brown flour in reserved drippings until light brown. Quickly stir in milk, water, salt and pepper. Bring to boil, stirring constantly. Add meatballs and reduce heat. Simmer, covered, about 30 minutes or until meatballs are cooked through, adding more water if needed. Serves 4.

Tender Barbecue Meatloaf

1½ pounds ground beef
1 egg, beaten
¼ cup milk
1½ teaspoons salt
2 slices bread, crumbled
1 small onion, chopped
¼ to ½ cup gold (mustard-based)
   barbecue sauce

Thoroughly combine ground beef, egg, milk, salt, bread and onion. Shape into a loaf and place in slow cooker. Top with barbecue sauce, and cover. Set on high and cook 1 hour, then turn to low and cook 8 to 9 hours. (This recipe may be doubled for a 5-quart slow cooker). Serve with white rice, carrots and collard greens.

Chris Bennett, West Columbia

This is an easy, great-tasting meatloaf.

Mom's Easy Sunday Spaghetti

1½ pounds ground beef
1 onion, chopped
½ to 1 cup chopped fresh mushrooms
    or 1 can diced mushrooms, drained
1 packet spaghetti sauce mix plus
    ingredients noted on packet,
    or 1 (18-ounce) jar spaghetti sauce
½ tablespoon Italian seasoning
2 teaspoons garlic powder
Water as needed
Salt and pepper to taste
Cooked spaghetti noodles

My mom made this recipe just about every Sunday. She would get the sauce cooking in a slow cooker in the morning. When we came home from church, we ate a great spaghetti meal. Sometimes she used her own seasonings, but most times she used a seasoning mix. Either way, it tasted homemade.

Brown ground beef and drain. Combine with remaining ingredients, except noodles, in a slow cooker. Cook on high about 2 hours. Add more salt and pepper, if needed. Serve sauce over cooked noodles or mix together.

Michael & Michelle Luetgens, Greenville

Lasagna

Sauce:

½ pound ground mild or hot
   sausage
1½ pounds ground beef
1 clove garlic, minced
½ tablespoon ground basil

1½ teaspoons salt
1 (16-ounce) can chopped
   tomatoes
2 (6-ounce) cans tomato paste
12 ounces (1½ cups) water

In a large pan, brown sausage and beef; drain. Add remaining ingredients and cook over medium heat 15 to 20 minutes. Remove from heat and set aside.

Filling:

3 cups ricotta cheese
½ cup grated Parmesan cheese
2 tablespoons parsley

2 eggs, beaten
2 teaspoons salt
½ teaspoon pepper

Combine Filling ingredients; mix well.

1 (10-ounce) package lasagna
   noodles, cooked al dente and
   drained

16 ounces grated mozzarella cheese

Spread a few tablespoons Sauce on bottom of deep 9x13-inch glass baking dish. Layer noodles over top of sauce. Spread a layer of Filling over noodles; sprinkle with mozzarella cheese. Repeat layers beginning with sauce, until all ingredients are used. Bake at 375° for 30 to 45 minutes. Allow to rest 5 to 10 minutes before cutting into squares. Serves 12.

Neil's Goulash

1 box large elbow macaroni or shells
  (I like the shells, they hold more juice)
1 pound ground chuck
1 medium white onion, chopped
1 bell pepper, chopped
1 (14.5-ounce) can diced tomatoes
1 (6-ounce) can tomato sauce
Chili powder to taste

This recipe is one of my daddy's (Neil Cost) favorites. It is just plain delicious and so, so easy! It only takes about 20 minutes from start to the table. It is great leftover too!

Prepare macaroni or shells according to package directions minus a few minutes, as they will get more cooking time in the pan. In a large pan, brown ground chuck; drain. Add onion and bell pepper; cook until tender. Add tomatoes and tomato sauce. Add chili powder. (The exact amount is unknown—Daddy said keep putting it in until the liquid looks like coffee. It's a pretty good amount.) Add cooked macaroni to the pan and cook on medium heat for about 10 to 15 minutes so flavors will blend together. Serve with bread and a salad. Feeds 4.

Sally Morris, Greenwood
www.RealEstateGreenwoodSC.com

Blue Ridge Mountains

Beth Whitcomb/istock/thinkstock

Randy's Easy Pizza Casserole

1 (14-ounce) jar pizza sauce, divided
1 (6-ounce) bag pepperoni slices, divided
Ground sausage and beef, browned,
   as much as you like, divided
Shredded pizza cheese, divided
1 (13.8-ounce) can refrigerated pizza crust dough

We make this recipe when we just don't want a normal pizza. You can't eat it like a sliced pizza; you'll need a plate, fork, and some napkins! But it tastes really good and you can use any ingredients you like.

Coat a 9x13-inch glass casserole dish with nonstick cooking spray. Add ½ sauce, ¾ pepperoni slices, ¾ browned meat and some cheese. Mix. Bake at 350° until hot, about 15 minutes. Roll out dough and place over top, being careful because it's hot. Cook about 10 minutes, or until it rises a bit. Then top with remaining sauce, meat and cheese as you would a pizza. Continue to bake until cooked and cheese is golden, about 30 to 40 minutes.

Randy Tumblin, Laurens

Rosewood Manor, Marion

Brian Nolan/istock/thinkstock

Porter Shepherd's Pie

2 tablespoons oil
6 tablespoons butter, divided
2 pounds ground beef
1 large onion, diced
2 cloves garlic, peeled and crushed
3 carrots, diced
1 (12-ounce) bottle Thomas Creek
    Porter
½ cup beef stock
1 teaspoon parsley
1 teaspoon thyme
1 teaspoon oregano
½ teaspoon sage
2 cups frozen peas
6 potatoes, cubed
Salt and pepper to taste
¼ cup milk
1 cup shredded Cheddar cheese
    (optional)

Preheat oven to 375°. In a large skillet, add oil and melt 2 tablespoons butter over medium-high heat; add beef and brown thoroughly. Remove beef; set aside. Add onion to skillet with a pinch of salt. Cook 5 minutes, then add garlic and carrots. After cooking an additional 10 minutes, add beef back to skillet.

Stir in Thomas Creek Porter and beef stock and bring to a simmer. Add parsley, thyme, oregano, sage and peas. Continue simmering 20 minutes.

While beef mixture is simmering, bring a large pot of water to a boil and add potatoes. Cook until fork tender, about 10 minutes. Remove from heat and drain. Add remaining 4 tablespoons butter, salt and pepper; mash evenly. Add milk and continue mixing until thoroughly combined.

Fill bottom of a 9x13-inch baking dish with beef mixture and cover with mashed potatoes. Bake 25 minutes. Remove from oven, cover with shredded Cheddar, if desired, and return to oven an additional 5 minutes. Enjoy!

Thomas Creek Conduplico Immundus Monachus, an imperial/strong porter beer, is the secret ingredient for this shepherd's pie. Use your favorite porter, or your favorite brew to adjust the flavor to your own taste.

Christopher McElveen
Thomas Creek Brewery, Greenville

Margaret Holmes
The South's Italian Beef

3 pounds top round
1 cup water
1 garlic bulb, cloves separated, peeled
2 tablespoons olive oil
⅓ cup chopped parsley
½ medium onion, diced
Hot sauce to taste
Roasted peppers to taste
1 (14.5-ounce) can Margaret Holmes
**   tomatoes, okra and corn**

If you've been around South Carolina and the South in general, you probably know about Margaret Holmes. The familiar name is on select canned foods found on grocery shelves far and wide. The cannery dates back to the early 1930s and was owned by Ed Holmes who, under the watchful eyes of his wife Margaret, began to can white acre peas and squash in his kitchen. Margaret was a very meticulous cook and only allowed the freshest, highest-quality vegetables into her kitchen. Being the true southern gentlemen that he was, Ed decided to name the product line after his wife. Over the years, the Margaret Holmes label became known for its commitment to quality, freshness, and taste. This recipe is a favorite and includes Margaret Holmes tomatoes, okra, and corn. Hope you enjoy it!

Place meat in a large skillet ; add water. Insert garlic cloves into meat, using small incisions. Drizzle with olive oil, then sprinkle with parsley. Top with onions. Cook on stove over medium heat for 3 to 4 hours until very tender. Add more water if needed. About ½ hour before done, drizzle with hot sauce; add roasted peppers and Margaret Holmes tomatoes, okra and corn.

Margaret Holmes Co. and McCall Co., Effingham
www.margaretholmes.com

The Piedmont Blues and Hash Bash
Abbeville • 2nd Week in October

If you love Piedmont blues music, hash, and slow-smoked barbeque, then the historic town of Abbeville, South Carolina is the place you will want to be the second weekend of October. The Piedmont Blues and Hash Bash will celebrate these great folklife South Carolina traditions on the historic town square. As the popularity of the festival grows, Abbeville is becoming a favorite annual stop for barbeque teams and hash artisans competing for top prize money and awards. Bring a blanket or chair, come out and enjoy traditional blues music and great food. It's fun for the whole family.

864.366.4600 • www.bluesandhash.com

Grandmother's Hash

1 pound stew beef or more
Water for stock
1 large onion
Mustard
Salt and pepper
Dash vinegar

Boil beef in a pot with water until well done. Reserve stock. Grind beef with onion using a hand or electric grinder set to a fine grind. Return ground beef with onion back to stock and add remaining ingredients to your taste. First, add mustard; you want the hash to have a yellow tinge. Then add salt and pepper and a little vinegar, be careful not to add too much vinegar or you will overpower the hash. Simmer, taste later and see what seasonings you may need to add. This hash will always be better the next day.

John S. Jones III, Blythewood

This hash recipe is at least three generations old. It has been passed down from my great grandmother. Adjust the amount of beef and ingredients according to how many people you are serving. Serve over rice or bread.

Barbeque Hash & "Wite" Rice

1 pound chicken livers, chopped fine
½ stick butter, divided
2 cups hash-brown potatoes
1 medium onion, chopped
4 pounds pulled pork, chopped fine
½ cup vinegar and pepper barbeque sauce
½ cup mustard barbeque sauce
6 cups water

This is a great South Carolina side dish that includes a state favorite...Hash! We are known for hash in South Carolina—it is unique to us. This recipe is for a time-honored favorite, Hash and "Wite" Rice. Hope you enjoy.

Sauté chicken livers in ¼ stick butter. Boil hash browns in water and mash with a potato masher. Sauté onion in remaining ¼ stick butter until soft. Combine all ingredients and simmer until ready to serve. Salt and pepper to taste. Serve over rice.

*Bronson "Bronnie" Smith, Columbia
Master Judge, South Carolina Barbeque Association
www.scbabarbeque.com*

Pickin' & Piggin' in the Park
Columbia • April/May

A world class barbeque cook-off & music celebration at Saluda Shoals Park! Savor the flavor of award winning 'Q' from South Carolina's best barbeque cookers while enjoying great live music from local bands! Barbeque tasting starts in the evening and goes until it runs out. Enjoy music from live bands all afternoon. Tickets are $10 per person/advance; $12 day of the event and $5 children 12 & under. For tickets & information call 772-1228 or visit www.icrc.net.

803.772.1228 • www.icrc.net

John's Hash for a Crowd

20 pounds pork shoulder or Boston butt
20 pounds beef chuck roast
15 pounds potatoes, peeled and diced
15 pounds onions, peeled and diced
2 pounds butter or to taste
Salt and pepper to taste

Hash recipes vary a good bit. Some seasonings that many South Carolinians use include mustard, tomato paste, ketchup, Worcestershire sauce, vinegar, and cayenne or Tabasco. I cook hash on a large scale! I usually cook 120 quarts on Memorial Day for family and friends. If you're making a large pot (at least 10 gallons) then I suggest that you try my method. Here's a quick tip: If you let it scorch and stick to the pot, your hash—and hard work—will be wasted.

Precook meat, covered in water, in large roasting pans at 225° or in a large table top roaster. I cook it overnight or until meat falls apart. Remove meat and pull out fat, bone and connective tissue. Pull meat apart into small portions. Pour leftover broth into large containers and allow it to cool. The fat will rise to the top and solidify. Remove fat and reserve broth. Refrigerate cooled meat and broth unless they are going straight to the hash pot. This seems like a lot of work, but it will save work later and give you a less fatty hash.

I suggest at least a 10-gallon cast iron pot for this recipe. Bring about 4 gallons water to a boil and add meat. Add more water if necessary to make sure meat has plenty of room to agitate and break down. Reduce heat to a simmer. Stir frequently and make sure meat has plenty of room to move around. As water cooks out you can add broth instead of water. Keep a close eye as you'll need to add liquid as needed. When meat starts to break down, about 2 hours, add potatoes and onions. Once you add these starches, you'll need a steady stir to keep it from sticking to the pot. Stir from the bottom. Let thicken (do not add liquid). You will need to stir more vigorously at this stage. Reduce heat if needed to prevent scorching. Cook until potatoes are soft and starting to cook away. Add butter, salt and pepper. Taste and add additional seasonings. The process after the precooked meat is added to the pot is about 6 to 7 hours and makes about 40 quarts.

John Waldrop, Abbeville
Senior Judge, South Carolina Barbeque Association

John's Slow Cooker Hash

1 (4- to 4½-pound) Boston butt roast
1 (1½- to 2-pound) beef chuck roast
Salt and cracked pepper to taste
3 large baking potatoes, peeled and diced
3 medium onions, peeled and diced
1 stick (½ cup) butter

Seasonings:

5 tablespoons white vinegar
2 tablespoons spicy brown mustard
1 tablespoon red pepper flakes
2 teaspoons cayenne pepper
4 tablespoons tomato paste
2 tablespoons Worcestershire sauce
Salt and cracked black pepper to taste

The original recipe from my grandmother's farm included beef, pork, and the occasional critter such as rabbit or turtle. I've simplified the recipe to create her hash in the slow cooker instead of a traditional cast iron pot. Grandmother's seasonings were mainly salt and pepper. The selected seasonings are only suggestions, please season as you like. Every South Carolina hash varies on the preference of the cook. Traditions vary greatly from region to region and often block to block.

Rub both roasts with salt and cracked pepper, then place in a 5-quart slow cooker. Add diced potatoes and onions, and fill slow cooker with hot water or stock and cover. Cook on high 6 to 7 hours until meat falls apart. Keep a check on the water level adding more as needed. Next, remove meat from the pot and pull apart to let cool. Remove the bone, fat and connective tissue. Pull meat apart into small pieces and then give it a light chop. Break up potatoes and onions in the pot with a potato masher. Return meat to the slow cooker. Still on high, let it cook another 4 hours. Add butter and reduce heat to lowest setting. Let it cook another 6 hours or until it is the consistency you like. The seasonings are a suggestion; season as you like. Add your seasonings 1 at a time and taste as you go. Serve over white rice or white bread. Hope you enjoy!

John Waldrop, Abbeville
Senior Judge, South Carolina Barbeque Association

ASC Greenway BBQ & Bluegrass
Fort Mill • September

There's music in the air and BBQ on your plate! Join us for live music on Dairy Barn lawn plus horse rides, wagon rides, kids' hay mazes, kayaking and canoeing, pedal karts, and more. Beverages, including beer and sodas, will be available for purchase. The cook teams will be competing in pulled pork and ribs. With your entry you will be able to taste BBQ from our teams as they battle for the trophy and bragging rights. This event is sanctioned by the Southern Barbecue Network. Admission is $10 for non-members, $8 for members. Music-only tickets are available for $5 per person.

803.548.7252 • www.ascgreenway.org

Mock Pork Back and Rice

3 pounds pork chops (not lean)
½ stick butter
2 onions, chopped (I prefer sweet)
1½ cups chopped celery
4 to 5 cups chicken stock
2 cups water
1 bunch green onions
1 teaspoon cayenne pepper
1 tablespoon Worcestershire sauce
3 bay leaves
1 tablespoon minced garlic
1½ teaspoons salt
1½ teaspoons pepper
4 cups white rice

In a skillet, brown pork in butter with onion and celery until edges are golden. Chop pork into small pieces or tear apart with a fork; discard bones. Transfer chopped pork, onion and celery to a stockpot and add remaining ingredients, except rice. Bring to a boil, then add rice. Cover, reduce heat and cook until rice is done. You can serve when water is absorbed or put everything into greased glass baking dishes and bake for about 20 minutes. Before serving, add some crunchy onions to the top, if desired.

C. Jacobs

Chorizo Stuffed Peppers

1 (8-ounce) package chorizo
1 (16-ounce) package lean ground beef
1 large onion, diced
1 (15-ounce) can stewed diced tomatoes
1 (16-ounce) bag 10-minute boil-in-bag
   rice
4 large green bell peppers, tops cut off
   and seeded
1 (8-ounce) package shredded Cheddar
   or Mexican blend cheese

Preheat oven to 350°. Brown chorizo, ground beef and onion until almost cooked. Combine with tomatoes and rice. Stuff peppers and bake 30 minutes in a baking dish. Top with cheese and bake an additional 5 minutes until cheese is melted.

Tiffany Lesniak, Charleston
The Navy Wives of
South Carolina Recipes

Because I rarely have extra time, I prefer to prep and precook everything. When it's time to serve, I mix everything together, stuff the peppers, and bake.

Pork Fest
Elloree • April

Held each April at Joe Miller Park in Elloree, Pork Fest is a hometown competition where teams throughout the community come to battle for bragging rights. Friday night is the popular Anything-but-Barbeque cook-off while Saturday is the barbeque competition. Judging is done by popular vote and a judges panel for both days of the event. Both events are open to the public for sampling while enjoying live music, a bake sale, and the wildly popular Pork Fest Pigs auction.

803.897.2821 • www.elloreesc.com

Daddy's "Turkey Calling" Ham Fried Rice

1 (28-ounce) box Minute Rice
1 center slice ham
1 bunch spring onions (or white onion),
    chopped (do not use sweet onion)
1 (14.4-ounce) can bean sprouts,
    drained well
3 eggs
Soy sauce to taste

My dad, Neil Cost, is a renowned turkey hunter and custom turkey call maker. He was dubbed "The Stradivarius of Turkey Call Makers" by Earl Mickel, author of Turkey Call Makers Past and Present. *Dad's calls are treasured and owned by turkey hunters all over the country, including some very well known celebrities and politicians. My parents entertained hunters from all over the country during turkey hunting season in Greenwood. They came to tune their calls and listen to the master, Neil Cost, recall turkey hunts and relay tips on how to best call up that elusive bird. They always asked for daddy's Ham Fried Rice when invited for dinner.*

Prepare rice according to package directions. Cut ham into small cubes and sauté in a saucepan in a small amount of oil. Add onions and bean sprouts. (If using a white onion, cook onion until tender before adding bean sprouts.) And 1 tablespoon water; cover and let steam a couple of minutes until bean sprouts and onions are slightly wilted. Beat eggs; add to pan and scramble. Add cooked rice and mix well. Add soy sauce. Feeds 4.

This recipe will only take about 15 to 20 minutes start to finish and is even better left over—so make extra! We always have garlic bread and a salad with it.

Sally Morris, Greenwood
www.RealEstateGreenwoodSC.com

Thomas Creek
Red Ale Pork Roast

1 (5-pound) pork shoulder roast
8 cloves garlic, peeled
2 large red onions, diced
4 large tomatoes, diced
2 (16-ounce) cans cannellini beans
1 (12-ounce) bottle Thomas Creek Red Ale
3 tablespoons chopped fresh rosemary
2 tablespoons chopped fresh thyme
2 tablespoons chopped fresh Italian parsley
Salt and pepper to taste

The flavor of the Thomas Creek Red Ale adds a rich, deep taste to the pork in this simple recipe. And you can't beat the spices involved—I think using fresh as possible adds more flavor. The lower and slower cooking time allows the aroma and taste of fresh thyme and rosemary really sink in! You will not believe how good this smells while it's cooking. Enjoy!

Preheat oven to 300°. Brown roast on all sides in a large skillet over medium-high heat. Allow roast to rest 10 minutes to reabsorb any lost juices. Use the tip of a small knife to plunge 1½ inches into the roast in 8 places around the roast; insert a garlic clove into each cut. Place roast in a large roasting pan. Add onions, tomatoes, beans and ale to the roasting pan. Season with rosemary, thyme and parsley, reserving some herbs for late in the cooking process so their color and aroma remain fresh. Cover dish and bake about 4 hours. Then, raise oven temperature to 425° and continue baking another 30 minutes. Uncover roast, sprinkle with remaining spices and continue baking an additional 30 minutes. Allow roast to rest, covered, for 15 minutes. Serve with rice and seasonal vegetables. Enjoy!

Christopher McElveen, Thomas Creek Brewery, Greenville

South Carolina Chitterlings

1 (10-pound) bucket fresh or frozen chitterlings
Cold water to cover
1 cup cider vinegar
5 bay leaves
2 large onions, coarsely chopped
2 large potatoes, peeled and coarsely chopped
1 green or red bell pepper, cored, seeded
   and coarsely chopped
3 cloves garlic, minced
Salt and freshly ground black pepper to taste
Hot pepper sauce

Chitlins take a lot of time and effort to clean. They are partially cleaned when they are sold in the store, but do require additional hand cleaning before they are ready to cook and eat. The secret to good, and safe, chitlins is in the cleaning, not in the cooking. When buying chitterlings, be prepared to buy 10 pounds of chitlins to get 5 pounds to cook.

If chitterlings are frozen, thaw before cleaning. Using a small soft brush, clean chitterlings thoroughly; rinse in several changes of cold water. Cut into 1½- to 2-inch pieces. Place cleaned chitterlings into a large pot; cover with water and vinegar. Add bay leaves, onions, potatoes, bell pepper, garlic, salt and pepper. Bring to a boil; turn heat to low and simmer 2½ to 3 hours or until chitterlings are tender. Remove from heat; drain well. Serve with your favorite hot pepper sauce.

South Carolina Department of Parks, Recreation & Tourism

Chitlin Strut
Salley • Saturday after Thanksgiving

The Chitlin Strut is one of the oldest festivals in the state of South Carolina. We have completed our 46th year. This event was started as a means of earning money to purchase Christmas decorations for the town. It is unique more from the standpoint that it "honors" hog intestines (chitterlings) as the main food item (fried or boiled). Other than this, it is much like any other festival with a parade, music, carnival, food concessions, and arts and crafts. The Chitlin Strut also has a hog calling contest and a Strut dance contest.

803.258.3485 • www.chitlinstrut.com

Pork Cutlets with Bourbon-Glazed Peaches and Onions over Creamy Grits

Creamy Grits:

1 cup heavy cream
3 cups water
1 cup grits

Salt and pepper to taste
1 (8-ounce) package cream cheese, softened

Bring cream and water to a boil. Stir in grits; season with salt and pepper. Reduce heat and simmer until cooked. Stir in cream cheese; check seasoning. Keep warm until ready to serve.

Oil
1 cup flour
Salt and pepper to taste
5 (6-ounce) pork cutlets cut from a pork tenderloin
½ red onion, sliced

2 tablespoons sugar, divided
6 South Carolina peaches, peeled, pitted and cut into eighths
6 ounces bourbon (such as Maker's Mark)
2 ounces cold butter

Heat oil in a sauté pan. Season flour with salt and pepper. Dredge pork cutlets in flour mixture and sauté pork until done. Set aside. Wipe out pan; add fresh oil. Drop in onion slices and season. As they start to cook, sprinkle with 1 tablespoon sugar. When sugar melts and onions begin to brown, add peaches. Add remaining tablespoon sugar and let caramelize. Add bourbon and flame off. Season and finish by swirling in cold butter.

To serve, place a bed of grits on a plate. Lean pork on grits. Top pork with peaches and onions.

Chef Robert Stegall-Smith, Florence
Corporate Chef, Institution Food House.
South Carolina Peach Council

John's South Carolina Slow Cooker BBQ

1 pork roast (loin butt or ends)
1 bottle BBQ sauce
1 to 2 tablespoons salt and pepper

This is an easy recipe for South Carolina shredded slow cooker BBQ with only a few ingredients. We all enjoy some good South Carolina BBQ— even in a slow cooker. You can add salt and pepper to taste, and I don't add any extra water or liquid. I just use my favorite brand of BBQ sauce. Give it a day, the slower the better.

Place roast in a slow cooker, no liquid added. Cover and cook on low 10 to 12 hours. Remove from slow cooker, remove grease and wipe inside of pot with paper towel. Shred meat or chop meat from bone. Place meat back into slow cooker. Pour BBQ sauce over meat and sprinkle with salt and pepper. Cover and cook on high 2 to 3 hours. Then it's ready to eat!

John S. Jones III, Blythewood

BBQ-Shag Festival
Hemingway • April

The South Carolina BBQ Shag Festival celebrates 25 years of family fun for everyone. In April, 10,000 to 15,000 people will join us for live music, the best fireworks show ever, a car show hosted by the Palmetto Cruisers, plus crafters and other vendors. There will also be plenty of fun for the kids with rides, pony rides, a petting zoo, face painting, and blow up inflatables. Our whole hog BBQ contest is one of the highest paying in the state with a $3000 first place prize ($1500 second place, $1250 third place, $1000 fourth place, and $750 for fifth place). Visit our website at www.scbbqshagfestival.org for history, info on the festival, and pictures from previous festivals.

843.344.2527 • www.scbbqshagfestival.org

Chef Chris Casner's Braised Beef Short Ribs

8 cut beef short ribs (bone in)
Salt and pepper to taste
1 cup diced celery
1 cup diced carrots
2 cups diced onions
4 cups red wine
2 cups beef stock
2 bay leaves

Pat beef dry and season with salt and pepper. Sear beef, meat side down, and add vegetables after 1 minute. Turn beef to sear on all sides while browning vegetables. Remove beef when browned on all sides. Add red wine, beef stock and bay leaves to vegetables. Reduce heat to medium-low and place beef back in pan. Cover and simmer 1 hour or until beef is tender. Remove beef and increase heat to medium-high. Allow sauce to reduce to approximately 2 cups or until slightly thickened. Add beef back to sauce and heat to serving temperature.

Chef Chris Casner
Just Eat This, Summerville

Randy's Dual Meat Barbecue

1 pork butt
1 beef roast or beef stew meat or tips
Salt and pepper to taste
Cajun seasoning to taste (optional)
1 to 2 green bell peppers, finely chopped
1 to 2 small onions, finely chopped
2 bottles hickory barbecue sauce

Smoke or bake meats in the same pan with a little bit of water and a light cover of foil. Shred meat when almost done and beginning to get tender. Continue to simmer in the juices to combine flavors. Add salt, pepper and Cajun seasoning (for more heat, if desired). When meat is just about fully cooked and tender, add chopped green peppers and onions. Drain excess fat and juice, then stir in barbecue sauce. Cover pan with foil, and continue to bake until sauce is heated through. Serve hot on fresh buns.

Randy Tumblin, Laurens

An Event to benefit FRIENDS of Caroline HOSPICE

Bands, Brews & BBQ

Port Royal • February

Bands, Brews & BBQ is held every February in downtown Port Royal. This event features a Wing Throw Down Party and a barbecue cook-off, sanctioned by the South Carolina BBQ Association, in the categories of Ribs & Butts. Join us to sample all you can eat of the best BBQ our area has to offer plus live music from local bands and entertainment for the children. It's great fun for the whole family and proceeds benefit Friends of Caroline Hospice, a charity that has provided loving care to Beaufort for over 30 years.

843.525.6257 • www.fochospice.org

Tomato Juice Barbecue Sauce

2 cups tomato juice
1½ tablespoons brown sugar
1½ tablespoons mustard
½ tablespoon celery salt
½ tablespoon cayenne
1 to 2 dashes black pepper
1 to 2 dashes paprika
1 to 2 dashes allspice
½ teaspoon Worcestershire sauce
¼ cup apple cider vinegar
1 tablespoon grated onion

Combine all ingredients in a small pot and stir until well mixed. Simmer over low heat about 30 minutes. Thin with water, or thicken with a bit of cornstarch, if needed. You may add ketchup, but it will add sweetness, so reduce amount of brown sugar.

Mike Hicks, manager,
and the hometown employees of
Southeastern Salvage, Columbia

Pepper & Vinegar Barbecue Sauce

1 cup cider vinegar
1½ teaspoons red pepper flakes
½ tablespoon salt
½ teaspoon cayenne pepper
1 to 2 tablespoons ketchup
1 tablespoon brown sugar

In a saucepan, stir together vinegar, red pepper flakes, salt and cayenne pepper. Bring to a boil. Stir in ketchup and brown sugar. Reduce heat to low, and simmer 30 minutes. Remove from heat and allow to cool. Store in a canning jar with a few cayenne peppers in the jar. If you aren't sealing jar with heat, refrigerate.

Mike Hicks, Go Gamecocks
Columbia

Here is a traditional South Carolina barbecue sauce. Many people call this a finishing sauce, serving it on the side and allowing the person eating it to decide how much they want to add to their plate of 'que.

Pig in the Park
Williamston • Weekend after Mother's Day

The Williamston Masonic Lodge No. 24 organizes this cook-off to help the Christian Learning Center and Operation Care and the Lodge. This also brings more people to our town.

864.934.4040 or 864.704.8131

Bronson's Eastern Vinegar & Pepper Barbeque Sauce

¾ cup chili powder
⅔ cup black pepper
2 tablespoons cayenne pepper
½ cup red pepper flakes
1 cup sugar

¾ cup kosher salt
1 cup ketchup
1 gallon cider vinegar, 5% acidity
1 gallon water

Add all spices to vinegar and water in a large stockpot. Slow boil at least 30 minutes.

Bronson "Bronnie" Smith, Columbia
Master Judge, South Carolina Barbeque Association
www.scbabarbeque.com

Greenville

Mike's Mustard Beer Barbecue Sauce

2 cups yellow mustard
2 to 3 ounces beer
⅓ cup apple cider vinegar
4 tablespoons brown sugar
1½ cups tomato purée
2 teaspoons Worcestershire sauce
½ tablespoon cayenne pepper
½ tablespoon black pepper
1 teaspoons garlic powder
½ teaspoon salt

Heat all ingredients in a saucepan over medium heat and mix well. Adjust for a thicker or thinner sauce, if needed. Use a bit of water to thin. Bring to a boil; as soon as it boils, remove from heat and allow to cool completely. Will keep for about a week covered in the fridge.

Mike Hicks, Columbia
Manager, Go Gamecocks

South Carolina–Georgia Border BBQ Cook-Off
Hardeeville • April

When Spring is in the air, you know it's that time of year when nothing tastes sweeter than a plate of barbecue. And the best barbecue by the best cooks along the state's border will return to Hardeeville in April for a tough competition. The Greater Hardeeville Chamber of Commerce hosts the South Carolina–Georgia Border Barbecue Cook-Off with big money prizes. Friday night starts the competition with local "celebrity" judges taste-testing chicken wings drizzled in sauces. Unlike other competitions, this one features four different sauces: pepper and vinegar, mustard based, and heavy or light tomato-based sauces, so come sample all. Join us and eat the best barbecue of South Carolina and Georgia at one festival.

843.784.3606 • www.hardeevillechamber.com

Bronnie's Mustard Barbeque Sauce

1 stick (½ cup) butter, melted
1 cup prepared mustard
½ teaspoon red pepper
1 tablespoon Coleman's dry mustard powder
1 tablespoon black pepper
1 cup apple cider vinegar
1 cup water
1 tablespoon sugar
1 tablespoon kosher salt

Part of the whole barbecue picture is sauce! This sauce is my personal favorite. Mustard-based barbeque sauces are unique to South Carolina. I usually smoke pork butts 12 to 15 hours over oak or hickory wood and serve with this sauce.

Combine all ingredients and whisk until smooth. Place in saucepan and cook over medium heat for 15 minutes. Pour into bowl and cover with plastic wrap until cool; this keeps a film from forming on top. Bottle and use on anything smoked.

Bronson "Bronnie" Smith, Columbia
Master Judge, South Carolina Barbeque Association
www.scbabarbeque.com

Valinda's Gullah Spice Seasoning

¼ cup ground celery seed
¼ cup paprika
¼ cup garlic powder
¼ cup onion powder
¼ cup ground black pepper
1½ teaspoons ground bay leaf
2 teaspoons ground ginger
1 teaspoon cinnamon
1 teaspoon allspice
½ teaspoon dry mustard powder
½ teaspoon salt

This is my very own Gullah seasoning. It was given to me years back by a neighbor when I was living near Charleston. I had no idea what Gullah food was, but I learned that it has a very rich culture and some amazing dishes. I hope you enjoy this recipe and I would encourage you not to change too much as it will affect the flavor.

Combine all ingredients in a bowl and mix. Transfer to a spice shaker. Use as you would any spice. It keeps for many months.

Valinda Davidson Wright & Family

Poultry

South Carolina Tailgate Chicken Tender Skewer, page 157

Sean's Chicken Bog

1 (4- to 5-pound) whole chicken
Salt and pepper to taste
1 pound ground hot or mild sausage
1 onion, chopped
1 (10¾-ounce) can cream of mushroom
soup
1 pound rice (uncooked)
1 pound smoked sausage, sliced ½-inch
thick

Place chicken in large stockpot with enough water to cover. Season with salt and pepper and boil about 1 hour. Remove chicken and set aside to cool; reserve broth.

In oven-proof stockpot or Dutch oven, brown ground sausage over medium heat. Add onion when sausage is almost done, and cook until sausage is done and onion is soft.

Skin and debone chicken and chop into bite-size pieces; add to sausage and onions. Add soup, rice, smoked sausage, salt and pepper; mix. Pour in enough reserved chicken broth to cover the mixture by about 2 inches. Cover pot and place in 350° oven for 1½ hours or until rice is cooked through.

Some of my fondest memories of my dad, Ron Shrum, are when we spent time together on the golf course. Dad was an avid golfer and a great cook, as was my mom. I would not have the appreciation and love for cooking, or for the game of golf, that I do now if it were not for my parents. My dad was a member of a golf club in Clinton called Musgrove Mill. Over many years I would meet him there for a few rounds on the weekends. We were often joined by my brothers and dad's friends. Dad moved to Johnson City, Tennessee, but he often came to visit and play golf in Charleston. We always enjoyed the trips.

There was always some type of function at Musgrove Mill that would include a pig roast or barbecue. One of the great dishes that was always on the menu was this Chicken Bog. Dad always asked for the recipe and on one trip he finally got it! He made it when I went home to visit one weekend and he gave me the recipe. This recipe has become a mainstay and favorite of my family and I'm always asked to make it for family and friends. I gladly accommodate and I always think about my dad and the many great rounds of golf we had together.

Sean Shrum, USCG retired, Charleston

Janet's Chicken Bog

The Regular Version:

1 large hen
1½ cups rice
1 onion, chopped

1 (14-ounce) package mild Hillshire
    Farms Sausage, sliced
Salt and pepper to taste

Boil hen in large stockpot in enough water to cover. Remove chicken from broth to cool, and spoon off fat from broth. Add rice and onion to broth. Cook until rice is done. Skin and debone chicken and chop. Pan-fry sausage until brown; drain. Add cut-up chicken and sausage to rice. Season with salt and pepper. Serve warm with my Broccoli Cornbread (page 26).

Healthier and Faster Chicken Bog for a Crowd:

5 (2-cup) bags boil-in-bag brown rice
2 (28-ounce) cans chicken stock
2 pounds chicken tenders
2 onions, chopped

2 (14-ounce) packages Hillshire Farms
    Sausage, sliced
Salt and pepper to taste

Boil rice bags according to package directions. Discard water. In large stockpot, combine chicken stock, chicken tenders and onions. Bring to a boil and cook until done. Remove chicken tenders and set aside to cool, reserving stock. Brown sausage; drain. Add cut-up chicken, sausage, and cooked rice to stock and onion mixture. Season with salt and pepper. Serve warm with my Broccoli Cornbread (page 26).

Janet Swope Wade, Aiken

Easy Baked Chicken Bog in a Cup

4 cups chopped cooked chicken
½ stick (4 tablespoons) butter
1 sweet onion, chopped
1 green bell pepper, chopped
1 cup cooked crumbled bacon
1½ cups cooked brown rice
1 (10½-ounce) can chicken broth
Salt and pepper to taste
Creole seasoning to taste
½ cup crushed breadcrumbs
    (optional)

This may be one of the easiest Chicken Bog recipes ever. The key is a single-serving oven-safe baking dish for each person. The rest is all done with leftovers and easy-to-grab ingredients. Chicken Bog is like chili in South Carolina. There are a zillion variations...this one is fast, easy, and full of flavor.

Preheat oven to 350°. In a skillet, heat chicken in butter to brown the edges and add a golden touch. Combine remaining ingredients, except breadcrumbs; add to skillet. Heat until warm. Spoon equal portions into individual baking dishes. Top with breadcrumbs, if desired. Bake until hot, about 15 minutes.

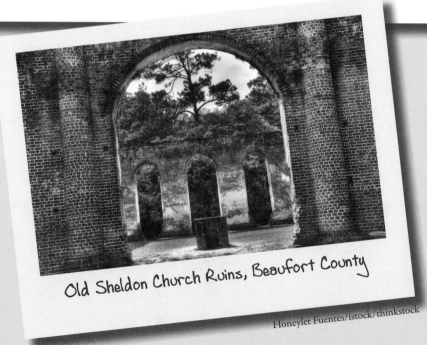

Old Sheldon Church Ruins, Beaufort County

Honeylet Fuentes/istock/thinkstock

Lowcountry-Style Chicken Purloo

6 slices bacon, diced
1 whole chicken, cut up
3 tablespoons vegetable oil (divided)
2 small onions, chopped (divided)
½ cup diced celery
2 cups long-grain white rice
2 (10½-ounce) cans chicken broth
Salt to taste
Freshly ground black pepper to taste
1 (14.5-ounce) can diced tomatoes,
    drained

Chicken Pilau, sometimes called Purloo, is a traditional South Carolina Lowcountry and Gullah chicken dish cooked with rice and bacon. There are many ways to make Chicken Purloo. The recipe can vary from family to family.

Cook diced bacon in a skillet. Remove bacon and drain.

In a large stockpot or Dutch oven, brown chicken in a small amount of oil. (Everything will finish in this pot, so its important to pick the right size.) Add chopped onions and celery; cook until soft. Stir in rice and brown the edges; don't burn the rice or fully cook it. Add just enough stock to cover; cook until chicken is done, about 45 to 60 minutes. Remove chicken and set aside to cool, then debone and pull meat apart.

Add pulled chicken and bacon back into pan; cook until rice is done. Before serving, add tomatoes and any additional seasonings you desire, cook for a few minutes to heat the tomatoes. Serve hot.

Miss B., Beaufort

Gullah Fried Chicken & Rice

1 fryer, cut-up
2 eggs, beaten
¾ cup buttermilk
Hot sauce to taste
Large dash garlic salt
Large dash black pepper
Large dash onion powder
1 cup flour
1 cup cornmeal
Lard or peanut oil for frying
1 package seasoned rice, cooked according
   to package directions

Gullah or Lowcountry recipes were passed down in the family by hand. Measurements were often left to memory. Available ingredients also played a part in preparation. If an ingredient was not available or not affordable, recipes were sometimes changed. This recipe uses prepared seasonings and spices but you can use fresh onion, garlic, and such, as you see fit.

Rinse chicken and pat dry. Whisk together eggs, buttermilk and hot sauce. Place garlic salt, black pepper, onion powder, flour and cornmeal in a clean paper grocery bag; shake to mix. Shake 1 to 2 pieces chicken in flour mixture at a time, then dip into egg wash. Shake chicken parts in flour mixture again to coat. Mix more flour as needed.

Fry chicken in an iron skillet in about 1 inch of lard or oil. Fry a few pieces at a time, making sure the chicken pieces don't touch. This helps to cook evenly. Brown chicken on both sides, then reduce heat to just a notch below medium. Continue frying until chicken is done. This will take about 25 minutes for larger pieces, while smaller pieces will be done sooner. Serve with rice.

South Carolina Poultry Festival

Batesburg-Leesville • 2nd Saturday in May

As a tribute to the largest employer in the region, the poultry companies, South Carolina Poultry Festival invites everyone to "Come Sample the South" in Batesburg-Leesville and to eggs-perience the eggs-cellent place to live, work, worship, and shop. At the festival, everyone will enjoy family entertainment and fun with a parade, six stages of live entertainment, contests, crafts, food vendors, a street dance, car show, fireworks, amusement rides, volleyball tournament, golf tournament, and a 5K road race. The festival proudly hosts the annual state 4H cooking contest, and everyone loves the "Cook-Cluck-Win-A-Buck" chicken cooking contest. South Carolina Poultry Festival—Almost 30 Years and Still Chickin' Lickin' Good!

803.532.4601 • www.scpoultryfestival.com

Geechee Stewed Chicken & Rice

1 pound cooked deboned chicken
Garlic powder, salt and black pepper
 to taste
1 (14-ounce) can chicken broth
⅓ cup minced onion
⅓ cup minced celery
Chopped green bell pepper to taste
Ground thyme to taste
2 tablespoons hot sauce
Rice (instant, regular or brown)

Brown chicken in a skillet with a bit of oil or butter. Season to taste with garlic powder, salt and pepper. Combine chicken with remaining ingredients, except rice, in a stockpot and simmer 30 to 45 minutes. While the chicken stews, prepare rice. When liquid has reduced to your liking, serve chicken mixture over rice in a bowl.

Geechee Broiled Chicken Quarters

2 tablespoons garlic powder
2 tablespoons onion powder
1 tablespoon salt
1 tablespoon pepper
1 tablespoon paprika
6 to 8 chicken leg quarters
Oil, egg white or milk

Combine seasonings in a bowl or bag. Dip chicken in oil, egg white or milk, then dredge, rub, or shake in the seasoning mixture. Bake or grill chicken until juices run clear. Serve with rice.

This variation of traditional Geechee chicken recipe is made for the oven or the grill instead of the fryer.

Jones Gap Falls, Jones Gap State Park, Greenville County

John Upchurch/istock/thinkstock

Hubby's Favorite Chicken and Artichoke Hearts

4 large chicken breasts, skinned, boned and pounded flat
⅓ cup flour
5 tablespoons butter
10 to 12 fresh mushrooms, sliced
1 (14-ounce) can artichoke hearts, rinsed, drained and halved
½ cup chicken broth
¼ cup white wine
Juice of ½ lemon or to taste
¼ teaspoon salt
⅛ teaspoon pepper

Sometimes you have to smile! This is my husbands' favorite... SERIOUSLY...all three of them! I have made this dish for ALL my husbands, even the two ex's. And I hear it is a favorite still. You have to laugh, because my ex's (we've remained friends) called asking for this recipe over the years. So, I have nicknamed it my "Elizabeth Taylor Recipe." I hope you enjoy it, and if you wish, it's easy to substitute veal cuts for the chicken.

Dredge chicken in flour, coating evenly. Heat butter in a large skillet. Sauté chicken until golden brown on all sides and cooked through. Transfer to a large heated plate. In the same skillet, sauté mushrooms about 2 minutes, then stir in artichoke hearts, broth, wine, lemon juice, salt and pepper. Cook over medium heat, stirring occasionally, until sauce is reduced slightly. Return cooked chicken to skillet to blend flavors. Serve hot when chicken is heated through.

Kassandra Britt DeFranco, Greenville

Oven-Fried Chicken and Peaches

½ cup crushed bran flakes
¼ cup sunflower seeds, chopped
½ teaspoon seasoned salt
¼ cup butter, melted
2 tablespoons lemon juice
4 to 6 chicken breast halves
4 South Carolina peaches, peeled,
    pitted and sliced in quarters

This is an easy oven-fried chicken recipe with a South Carolina peach twist. The secret is the two part "crunchy" dipping process! It's also very good with pork chops!

Combine crushed bran flakes, sunflower seeds and seasoned salt. In another dish, combine melted butter and lemon juice. Dip chicken pieces in butter mixture, then in bran mixture to coat evenly. Mix together remaining butter and bran flakes mixtures. Stir in peaches.

Place chicken in baking pan and bake at 350° for 30 minutes. Then add peach mixture and continue to bake another 30 minutes.

South Carolina Peach Council

Johnston Peach Blossom Festival
Johnston • 1st Weekend in May

Johnston Peach Blossom Festival has celebrated 30 years of food, fun, and fellowship. The celebration begins early with a beauty pageant the month before and a parade which starts at 10:30 the morning of the festival. Festival weekend kicks off with a Friday night dance. Saturday's food, crafts, rides for small kids, and local entertainment all day offer guaranteed fun for the whole family. We hope to see you there.

803.275.2345
www.johnstondevelopmentcorp.org

AwakenedEye/istock/thinkstock

Bourbon-Laced
Tipsy Chicken with Peaches

4 chicken leg quarters (thighs
    attached)
Salt and pepper to taste
2 tablespoons butter
1 large white or yellow onion, finely
    chopped
1 teaspoon paprika
1½ cups chopped green onion

½ cup orange juice
2 tablespoons bourbon
1 cup chopped fresh peaches (about 2
    medium peaches)
Nutmeg to taste
Additional chopped green onion for
    garnish

Preheat oven to 400°. Sprinkle chicken with salt and pepper. Place in 9x13-inch baking pan and set aside. In medium skillet, melt butter over medium heat. Add white onion and cook, stirring occasionally, until translucent, about 5 minutes. Add paprika and green onions; cook an additional 4 minutes. Spread onion mixture evenly over chicken, drizzle orange juice and bourbon over top. Bake 30 minutes, turning and basting occasionally. Remove from oven and spoon peaches over top. Sprinkle with nutmeg, and cook an additional 15 to 20 minutes or until chicken is tender, showing no trace of pink near the bone. Remove chicken from pan, place on serving dish and pour juices on top. Garnish with green onions and serve immediately.

Dori Sanders, author
South Carolina Department of Parks, Recreation & Tourism

Heather's Skillet Chicken Parmesan

6 tablespoons grated Parmesan cheese, divided
1½ cups Italian spaghetti sauce
6 skinless, boneless chicken breast halves
1½ cups shredded part-skim mozzarella cheese
Bowtie pasta, cooked al dente

As a Navy wife I started the Navy Wives of South Carolina Recipes database for all of my Navy spouse friends. It's a way we can swap good recipes, share cost-saving meal tips, and enjoy some fellowship. The database turned into a blog, and then a facebook page. It's all about being there for each other. This recipe is a great starting point for a meal, and then you can add what you wish, or what you have in the fridge.

Stir 4 tablespoons Parmesan cheese into spaghetti sauce. Coat a 12-inch skillet with cooking spray and heat over medium-high heat for 1 minute. Add chicken and cook 10 minutes or until well browned on both sides. Pour sauce mixture over chicken, turning to coat with sauce. Reduce heat to medium. Cover and cook 5 minutes or until chicken is cooked through. Top with mozzarella cheese and remaining 2 tablespoons Parmesan cheese. Let stand 5 minutes or until cheese melts. Serve over pasta.

Heather Steele, Charleston
The Navy Wives of South Carolina Recipes

olgakr/istock/thinkstock

South Carolina Tailgate Chicken Tender Skewers

1 pound chicken tenders
1 cup mustard barbecue sauce

2 tablespoons apple cider vinegar
Salt and pepper to taste

Place chicken in a plastic bag or between sheets of wax paper and flatten with a meat hammer. Marinate in remaining ingredients at least 30 minutes. Place on skewers and grill or bake until juices run clear.

Oven Barbecued Chicken

¼ cup water
¼ cup vinegar
3 tablespoons vegetable oil
½ cup ketchup
1 teaspoon mustard

3 tablespoons Worcestershire sauce
1½ teaspoons salt
½ teaspoon pepper
2 tablespoons chopped onion
1 chicken, cut up

Combine all ingredients, except chicken, in a saucepan and simmer 10 minutes. Pour over chicken in a 9x13-inch baking dish and bake at 350° for 1 hour or until chicken is done.

White Wine Linguine Chicken with Blackened Tomatoes

4 fresh tomatoes, sliced
⅓ cup butter
2 (10¾-ounce) cans cream of
    mushroom soup
1 packet Italian salad dressing mix
1 tablespoon minced garlic

⅔ cup white wine
4 ounces cream cheese
2 green onions, finely chopped
6 boneless, skinless chicken breasts
1 (16-ounce) package linguine pasta
Parmesan cheese

Spread tomatoes evenly on a cookie sheet. Broil until edges are brown, but not burned. Turn, to blacken other side.

While tomatoes are broiling, prepare cream cheese sauce. Melt butter in large pot. Stir in soup, dry dressing mix, garlic, wine, cream cheese and green onions until well-blended. Cook about 8 minutes over low heat, but don't let it boil. The sauce should be creamy and cream cheese should be melted and not lumpy.

When tomatoes are ready, set oven to 325°. Place chicken in a single layer in a 9x13-inch baking dish and pour cream cheese mixture evenly over chicken. Bake about 45 minutes or until chicken is done.

Cook linguine according to package directions; drain. Serve topped with chicken and sauce. Top with blackened tomatoes and Parmesan cheese.

Zesty Tailgate Grilled Wings

1 cup zesty Italian salad dressing
Dash honey
¼ cup barbecue sauce
16 chicken wings and drummies
Green onions, chopped
Parsley flakes

This is a perfect chicken wing recipe that can be cooked on the grill or even baked in the oven. Perfect for tailgating at football games or at home with the game on the radio or TV!

Combine salad dressing, honey and barbecue sauce in a bowl. Mix well, then add chicken. Cover, chill and marinate for an hour or so. Toss a few times to make sure everything is evenly coated. Grill chicken over medium-high heat, about 8 minutes on each side, until done. Brush with fresh barbecue sauce during the last minute or two of grilling. Before serving, sprinkle with onions and parsley.

Jay Williamson, Gamecock tailgater

Wingfest
Shelter Park Cove • Hilton Head
End of March

Around 20 local restaurants cook up their best wings. Your vote counts in the people's choice award. All day there is live music and so many more activities for the whole family. All proceeds benefit the Hilton Head Island Recreation Association's Children's scholarship fund.

843.681.7273 • www.islandreccenter.org

Carolina Citrus Geechee Wings

20 chicken wings, drummies or legs
2 cups orange juice
⅓ cup low-sodium soy sauce
2 tablespoons honey
Black pepper to taste
Dash celery powder

A great recipe for grilled chicken wings that can also be prepared in the oven. Since this recipe has roots from the beaches of South Carolina the use of a fryer is not suggested, but not ruled out. Coastal cooking took place over low fires that were blocked from the wind. Grilled, broiled or baked is the way to go. But if you must use a fryer then consider dredging the wings in a very light coating of cornmeal for a more traditional taste.

Wash chicken and set aside. In large bowl, combine remaining ingredients and mix well. Add chicken wings, cover and marinate 2 hours. Grill (or bake at 350°), turning as needed, until golden and the juices run clear.

Viktorija Kuprijanova/istock/thinkstock

Dad's Recipe Grilled Wings

2 pounds chicken wings
⅓ cup low-fat Italian dressing
Salt and pepper (or your favorite dry rub) to taste
1 stick (½ cup) butter, melted
⅓ cup balsamic vinegar
¼ cup soy sauce
1 cup Dad's Recipe BBQ Sauce

Place chicken in a 1-gallon zip-close bag, pour in Italian dressing and shake to coat. Remove chicken and season individual pieces with salt and pepper. Combine melted butter, vinegar and soy sauce. Grill wings over a medium fire, turning every 10 to 15 minutes. Baste often with butter mixture until done (a turkey baster works well). When wings come off grill put into a clean zip-close bag, add Dad's Recipe BBQ Sauce and shake to coat. Serves 4 or 5.

This recipe was concocted at a dove shoot at Inman on opening day. Over the years every man there, including the young boys that are now grown men with families, has taken credit for developing the best chicken wings you'll ever taste. The hunter that was supposed to bring the turkey fryer, peanut oil, etc., to cook the wings in the traditional manner didn't show. He used the "lame" excuse of his wife going into labor and having to go to the hospital! We had a huge grill on hand for cooking ribs and Boston butts... and we had wings, with no way to fry them as planned. So, we decided to pop the wings on the grill and make use of it. We had the other ingredients on hand and that's how "Dad's Recipe Grilled Wings" was born!

Holly Gillis, Simpsonville
www.dadsrecipe.com

Carolina Cream Cheese Chicken Packs

2 cups chopped cooked chicken
3 ounces cream cheese, softened
1 tablespoon chopped chives
2 tablespoons milk
Salt to taste
2 (8-count) packages refrigerated crescent rolls
¼ cup melted margarine
½ cup crushed seasoned crouton crumbs

In medium-size bowl, combine chicken, cream cheese, chives, milk and salt. Mix gently and evenly. Unroll crescent rolls and press together along perforations, making 4 rectangles. Place ¼ cup chicken mixture in center of each rectangle. Fold dough over filling. Pinch edges to seal tightly. Dip each packet in melted margarine and coat with crouton crumbs. Place on baking sheet and bake at 350° for 20 minutes or until golden brown.

Fish & Seafood

**Buttermilk Dredged Catfish,
page 171**

Meg's Georgetown Gourmet Grouper

¾ cup grated Parmesan cheese
½ cup butter, softened
3 tablespoons mayonnaise
3 tablespoons chopped green onions
2 teaspoons chopped fresh chives
6 (8-ounce) grouper fillets, about
    1-inch thick
¼ cup lemon juice
¼ teaspoon pepper
Lemon slices and fresh chives for
    garnish (optional)

Combine first 5 ingredients in a bowl and set aside. Place grouper on a lightly greased broiler pan rack. Drizzle lemon juice over fillets; sprinkle with pepper. Broil 6 inches from heat 8 to 10 minutes or until fish flakes when tested with a fork. Remove from oven; spread mayonnaise mixture on top of fillets. Broil an additional 1 to 2 minutes until cheese is lightly browned and bubbly. Do not cook cheese topping too long as grouper may dry out. Garnish with lemon slices and fresh chives.

Meg Tarbox, Georgetown

This is my all-time favorite recipe. Just about any firm white fish fillets will work. I keep the mayonnaise mixture on hand in the refrigerator at all times! Bon Appetit, Y'all!!!

Shuckin' in the Park
Moncks Corner • 2nd Weekend in March

It is never too early to mark your calendars for the Annual Shuckin in the Park Oyster Roast. There will be activities for the children including a jump castle. Food tickets can be purchased inside the gate. Entertainment will feature beach music, oldies, and popular songs. Small coolers are allowed but PLEASE no pets or golf carts.

843.899.5200 • www.oldsanteecanalpark.org

Cracker-Crusted Scamp Grouper

1 pound fingerling potatoes (or other small potato)
2 large leeks
1 large sweet onion
1 clove garlic
3 tablespoons butter, divided
Salt and pepper to taste
1 bunch fresh parsley
1 tablespoon oil, plus more for frying
2 cups oyster crackers
4 (7-ounce) fillets fresh scamp grouper
1 pint (about 30) fresh shucked oysters
1 pint half-and-half
Dash Tabasco
Dash paprika

Wash potatoes and place on sheet pan, season with salt and roast at 400° until tender, about 30 minutes.

Wash leeks well, then cut in half and slice thin. Peel onion, halve and slice thin. Peel and mince garlic. Heat 2 tablespoons butter in a saucepan; add leeks, onion and garlic. Season to taste with salt and pepper; cover. Cook over low heat 20 minutes or until very tender.

Wash parsley, pick leaves and purée in blender with 1 tablespoon oil and 1 tablespoon water.

Crush oyster crackers in blender, season with salt and pepper. Dredge fish in crackers to completely cover. Heat oil in sauté pan. Sauté grouper on both sides to golden brown. Finish in oven if not cooked completely.

Right before serving, heat 1 tablespoon butter in pan. Add drained oysters and cook just until edges curl. Add half-and-half, Tabasco and paprika; bring just to a simmer.

To plate, divide potatoes in center of 4 large bowls, spoon onion mixture over potatoes, then place fish on top. Spoon oyster stew around, then drizzle with puréed parsley. Serve immediately.

South Carolina Department of Parks, Recreation & Tourism

Chef Sandifer's Gulf Grouper 2 Ways

This dish showcases how southern and French foods can complement each other—the simplicity goes beyond tantalizing the taste buds with the heat of the blackened and cooling/neutralizing cream of the poached.

#1 - Blackened Grouper

Blackening Spice:

1 part Cajun Spice Blend   ½ part sugar
1 part Dry Jerk Spice Blend

Combine mixes and sugar. You can make your own spice blends or buy them, but be sure the spices are fresh, as it makes all the difference.

Cajun Spice Blend:

5 tablespoons paprika   1 tablespoon black pepper
3 tablespoons chili powder   1 tablespoon ground oregano
3 tablespoons salt   1 tablespoon cayenne
2 tablespoons onion powder

Dry Jerk Spice Blend:

2 tablespoons granulated garlic   1 teaspoon black pepper
2 teaspoons thyme   ½ teaspoon ground nutmeg
1 teaspoon ground allspice   ¼ teaspoon cinnamon
1 teaspoon ground habanero or   ¼ teaspoon ground cloves
  cayenne pepper

For Blackened Grouper:

1 (3-ounce) grouper fillet   ½ to 1 cup crawfish tail meat
2 tablespoons butter   Pinch sugar
1 leek, top and root discarded, split,   Pinch salt
  washed and sliced thin

Heat cast iron skillet to medium heat. Season fish fairly heavily on both sides with Blackening Spice. Cook thoroughly, turning heat down if it begins to smoke too much. In separate pan, melt butter and add leeks; sauté on medium until lightly brown (caramelized). Add crawfish and a pinch of sugar and salt; toss. Keep everything warm while preparing Poached Grouper.

#2 - Poached Grouper

Cream Sauce:

½ pound thick cut bacon, diced
1 shallot, peeled and minced
1 tablespoon flour
1 pint heavy cream

2 cups fresh green peas, blanched
Salt to taste
1 teaspoon white pepper

In a heavy bottom pan, render bacon over medium heat until cooked and slightly crispy. Add shallot and cook in bacon fat 2 minutes. Add flour, making a light roux. Add heavy cream, peas, salt and pepper. Continue cooking over medium heat until sauce thickens slightly.

For Poached Grouper:

2 cups vegetable stock
1 cup white wine
½ lemon, juiced

½ onion, chopped
1 (3-ounce) grouper fillet

In a separate saucepan, bring stock, wine, lemon juice and onion to a boil, then reduce to a light simmer, 160° to 170° Completely submerge fish in poaching liquid and cook until done. Be careful removing as fish will be very delicate if cooked correctly!

Serve 1 blackened and 1 poached grouper on same plate topped with their accompanying sauce.

Geoffrey D. Sandifer, Governor's Mansion Executive Chef

Class Five Fish Tacos with Spicy Mayo

Beer Batter:
¾ cup all-purpose flour
¼ cup cornmeal
2 tablespoons cornstarch
½ teaspoon salt (optional)
1 teaspoon baking soda
1 egg
1 cup Class Five IPA beer

I tried fish tacos once and decided that our Class Five IPA beer from Thomas Creek Beer would be a perfect ingredient for a tasty batter. Class Five is a term used in rafting and IPA stands for India Pale Ale. Hope you enjoy the recipe.

Combine dry ingredients in medium bowl. Blend egg and beer until mixture is smooth and egg is thoroughly incorporated. Quickly stir dry mixture into egg and beer mixture (batter may be lumpy).

Oil, for frying
1 pound firm whitefish (cod or halibut)
Flour to coat fish
8 tortillas (flour or corn)
Thomas Creek Spicy Mayo to taste
   (recipe on next page)
1 cup shredded cabbage

1 cup shredded red cabbage
1 avocado, sliced into eighths
1 medium carrot, shredded
Cilantro and lime wedges for garnish
Salsa (optional)
Sour cream (optional)

Preheat oil to 375°. Cut whitefish into 8 (2-ounce) strips. Lightly flour fish strips and dip in Beer Batter. Fry until golden brown; remove and drain excess oil on paper towels. You may lightly fry or bake tortillas, but avoid making them too flaky as they may fall apart. Place desired amount of Thomas Creek Spicy Mayo on tortilla, followed by a portion of whitefish, cabbage, red cabbage, avocado and carrots. Garnish with cilantro and lime wedges. Offer salsa and sour cream, if desired.

Christopher McElveen, Thomas Creek Brewery, Greenville

Flopeye Fish Festival

Great Falls • Memorial Day Weekend

On Memorial Day weekend of each year, the Flopeye Fish Festival means community-wide fun and recreation for locals and visitors. With a variety of food, fun and entertainment, along with the enthusiasm of homecoming atmosphere, the Flopeye Fish Festival attracts visitors from many states. The event brings our citizens together and preserves the saying, "After all, life is to enjoy."

803.482.6029 • www.flopeyefishfestival.com

Thomas Creek Spicy Mayo

⅓ cup plain yogurt
⅔ cup mayonnaise
2 tablespoons chopped cilantro
½ teaspoon chopped oregano
½ teaspoon cayenne pepper
½ teaspoon ground cumin
1 jalapeño, minced (seeds optional)
½ lemon, juiced
½ lime, juiced

Combine yogurt and mayonnaise. Add cilantro, oregano, cayenne, cumin and jalapeño; mix well. Juice lemon and lime into separate bowl; add mixture to mayonnaise until desired consistency is achieved. Enjoy!

Christopher McElveen
Thomas Creek Brewery, Greenville

Try this mayo on all kinds of things!

Creole Catfish

5 catfish fillets
1 small onion, diced
1 red bell pepper, diced
1 stalk celery, diced
⅓ cup water
1 chicken bouillon cube
1 small (4-ounce) can sliced mushrooms
1½ cups tomato juice
Salt and pepper to taste

Preheat oven to 350°. Rinse fish fillets and lay in a 9x13-inch glass baking dish. Cover with remaining ingredients. Back until fish is white and flaky, about 1 hour and 15 minutes, do not overcook.

Hardeeville Catfish Festival
Hardeeville • 3rd Weekend in September

Hardeeville hosts the two-day Hardeeville Catfish Festival the third weekend in September each year. This is a family event with a beauty pageant each summer. Mr. Whiskers, our resident catfish, invites you to come out to enjoy live entertainment, rides for the young and not-so-young, GREAT food, and a fantastic variety of vendors to shop from! Please go to our website for applications to participate. Check out our Facebook page for more information and lots of pictures!

843.784.3606 • www.hardeevillecatfishfestival.org

Buttermilk Dredged Catfish

1 teaspoon minced garlic
½ teaspoon ground cayenne pepper
½ teaspoon black pepper
½ teaspoon Italian seasoning
Buttermilk
6 to 8 catfish fillets
Oil for frying
½ cup flour
½ cup cornmeal
½ teaspoon onion powder
Dash salt and pepper

This is my recipe for dredged catfish. It also works great on pork chops, chicken tenders, and more.

In a bowl, combine garlic, cayenne pepper, black pepper and Italian seasoning with enough buttermilk to coat fillets. Add fillets, cover and refrigerate 3 hours to let the flavor soak in (turn fish at least once while soaking).

Heat oil in a fryer or skillet over medium heat. Combine flour, cornmeal, onion powder, salt and pepper. Dredge marinated catfish in flour mixture (discard marinade). Fry until golden brown on both sides.

Miss B., Beaufort

Tommy Bahama Ahi Tuna Poke

Tuna Poke Dressing:

⅓ cup sesame oil
⅓ cup soy sauce
¾ tablespoon minced fresh ginger
¾ tablespoon chipotle pepper paste
1 lime, halved and juiced
1 tablespoon minced shallot
4 teaspoons finely chopped cilantro
4 teaspoons finely chopped parsley
4 tablespoons capers

Combine all ingredients well and set aside.

This recipe is FIRST PLACE winner of the 2010 Myrtle Beach Taste of the Town. It has been on the Tommy Bahama menu for over 5 years. Fan outrage over a recent decision to remove this dish from the menu resulted in a quick change of heart. It's easy to make and the impressive presentation will draw rave reviews from all your guests.

Guacamole:

2 avocados, pitted, skinned and diced ¼-inch
½ cup finely diced yellow onions
1 jalapeño, stemmed, seeded and minced
1 cup small-diced ripe tomato

2 limes, halved and juiced
¼ cup chopped cilantro
½ cup bias-cut ¼-inch green onions
Pinch cayenne pepper
2 teaspoons kosher salt
1 teaspoon coarse ground black pepper

Combine all ingredients well and set aside.

Tuna:

½ pound ahi tuna steak, cut into ¼-inch cubes
8 ounces Tuna Poke Dressing
3 cups Guacamole

8 cilantro sprigs
40 pieces flatbread, crackers or wontons

To plate, combine tuna and dressing; toss well to coat evenly. Use 2½-inch wide by 3-inch tall ring molds (or a small empty tomato paste can, both ends removed and thoroughly cleaned). Build the molds starting with 1½ ounces guacamole. Add 1½ ounces tuna, then an additional 1½ ounces guacamole. Finish with 1½ ounces tuna. Gently remove ring mold, garnish with cilantro, and Voila! Loki Loki Tuna Poke. Serve with crisp tortilla chips, flatbread, or crispy wontons. Serves 8.

Tommy Bahama's Restaurant & Bar, Myrtle Beach

Taste of the Town
Myrtle Beach • Mid-October
(Always on a Tuesday)

Poised as the Grand Strand's largest culinary and social event of the year, and Myrtle Beach's premier food festival, this year's Taste of the Town will include over 50 area restaurants offering samples from their menus. Event to be held at The Myrtle Beach Convention Center:

843.448.6062 • www.TOTMB.com

Coastal Crab Fritters

2 cups crumbled crabmeat
2 eggs, beaten
1 teaspoon Old Bay seafood seasoning
½ cup milk
1 teaspoon salt
1 tablespoon sugar
1 cup sifted all-purpose flour
2 tablespoons oil for frying

Crumble crabmeat into corn-kernel sized pieces (you don't want the pieces too big). Combine crab with all ingredients, except oil, in a bowl and mix well. Add additional flour or milk, as needed. Drop spoonfuls of batter in hot oil in a skillet. Brown until golden. Recipe may be doubled.

Miss B., Beaufort

For this very easy recipe, fresh crabmeat from the crabbers at local markets is best. There are many places along the South Carolina coast where you can find fresh seafood, but you can use canned or imitation crab in a pinch. Try this recipe for corn fritters, shrimp fritters, crawdad fritters, and more. Just substitute the main ingredient of your choice for the crab. For added flavor, fry in bacon drippings instead of oil.

Charleston's Egg Breaded Crab Cakes

1 pound lump crabmeat
½ cup mayonnaise
2 green onions, finely chopped
½ cup finely chopped red bell pepper
2 teaspoons hot sauce
2 teaspoons Worcestershire sauce
1 egg, beaten
½ cup milk
½ cup coarse breadcrumbs
½ tablespoon seafood seasoning
½ ounce lemon juice

In a bowl, combine crabmeat, mayonnaise, onions, red bell pepper, hot sauce and Worcestershire sauce; form into ping-pong-ball-sized crab cakes. In a separate bowl, combine egg and milk. Dip crab cakes in egg mixture and coat with breadcrumbs. Sprinkle with seafood seasoning. Cook in a small amount of butter, oil or olive oil. (Do not use too much oil, just enough to cook and to brown.) Cook until golden brown and serve hot with a splash of lemon juice.

Karen Burns, Charleston

World Famous Blue Crab Festival
Little River • May

The purpose of this festival is, and will continue to be, one that supports and showcases the fabulous atmosphere of the local Little River Community, North Myrtle Beach and the entire Grand Strand area. You will experience arts and crafts vendors, food vendors, live music, a kids area, and lots of family fun. We encourage you to be a part of this tradition and join us for our World Famous Blue Crab Festival, on the Waterfront in Little River.

803.795.9755 • www.bluecrabfestival.org

Stone Crab Claws with Mustard Sauce

Captain Bobby and I enjoy sharing our "stonie" recipe! Kimberly's Crabs supplies only the freshest soft shell and stone crabs to the best local restaurants —Shawn Brock of Husk Restaurant in Charleston, Mike Lata of FIG Restaurant and many others. We love seafood and hope you enjoy this simple recipe for cooking fresh stone crab claws.

Stone Crab Claws:

1 to 2 pounds stone crab claws
Lukewarm water

In a stockpot, cover crab claws with lukewarm water and bring to a boil. Boil 8 minutes, not 10. Drain and run under cold water for a few minutes. Place on a cookie sheet and let crab claws stand 10 to 15 minutes. If you put them on ice too quickly before cooking, the meat will stick to the shell. Serve with Joe's Famous Mustard Sauce (see recipe on opposite page) or clarified butter.

Joe's Famous Mustard Sauce:

1 cup mayonnaise
1 tablespoon dry mustard, or to taste
2 teaspoons Worcestershire sauce
1 teaspoon steak sauce
½ cup heavy cream or milk
Pinch salt

In a small mixing bowl, whisk together all ingredients until blended and creamy. Cover and chill until serving. Enjoy!

Kimberly Carroll, Kimberly's Crabs, Mount Pleasant

South Carolina Cheesy Shrimp and Vegetables

1 (10¾-ounce) can cream of
    mushroom soup
½ cup milk
3 to 4 cups frozen broccoli, thawed
    (or other vegetables)

2 cups frozen salad shrimp, thawed
Salt and pepper to taste
Provolone cheese slices
1 (2.8-ounce) can French fried onions
Chopped fresh parsley for garnish

Combine soup, milk, broccoli, shrimp, salt and pepper in a 2-quart baking dish coated with nonstick cooking spray. Bake at 350° for 20 to 25 minutes. Arrange cheese slices on top, then sprinkle with fried onions. Bake another 5 to 10 minutes until cheese melts and starts to brown slightly. Serve hot with a garnish of parsley or parsley flakes.

Tip: Use shredded cheese, combine with fried onions, and spread evenly over the top.

Mark Walker, Clemson University Football fan, Clemson

Charleston Harbor, Mount Pleasant

Town of Mount Pleasant
Blessing of the Fleet & Seafood Festival
Mount Pleasant • Last Sunday in April

Since 1987, the Blessing of the Fleet and Seafood Festival has highlighted the importance of the local shrimping and fishing industry in Mount Pleasant. Seafood lovers come from all over the country to enjoy a boat parade and blessing of the shrimp/fishing fleet, savory seafood samplings sold by some of Mount Pleasant's best restaurants, live music, an arts/crafts show and Mount Pleasant Artists Guild Exhibit, shag and shrimp-eating contests, and family-friendly activities. Admission, activities, and parking are free!

843.884.8517 • www.ComeOnOverMP.com

Adluh's Carolina Breaded Shrimp

1 pound South Carolina shrimp, shelled and deveined
½ cup buttermilk
Dash hot sauce
Adluh Carolina Breader mix
Lemon juice (optional)

Dip shrimp in buttermilk mixed with a dash of hot sauce. Evenly coat with Adluh Carolina Breader and fry in a deep fat fryer at 325° to 350° or in a frying pan until golden brown. Serve with a splash of lemon juice, if desired.

Frank Workman, Columbia
Adluh Flour, www.adluh.com

Seafood has been part of the South Carolina diet since, well, since before there was even a South Carolina! We are known for every kind of seafood you can think of prepared in just about any manner you can imagine. But we like simple and traditional! Carolina Breader mix is a complete mix which means that no additional spices or ingredients need to be added...unless you want some extra heat with some hot sauce! The mix is "table tested" and can be used for all kinds of seafood, chicken, pork or vegetables. It includes wheat flour, enriched yellow cornmeal, salt, spices and coloring. Adluh Flour has been around since 1900 in South Carolina and we know our seafood and shrimp, as well as grits, flour, biscuits, muffins, breads...well, we just love good food.

Pete's S.C. Marinated Shrimp

1 green onion, sliced or chopped
2 tablespoons olive oil
2 tablespoons fresh lemon juice
2 tablespoons prepared horseradish
2 tablespoons seafood sauce or ketchup
1 tablespoon finely chopped chives
1 teaspoon hot pepper sauce
1 clove garlic, smashed
1 teaspoon Dijon mustard
Dash salt
2 pounds medium shrimp, cooked,
    peeled and deveined

For marinade, combine all ingredients, except shrimp, in a large bowl. Mix well. Add shrimp and toss to coat, or combine marinade and shrimp in a zip-close bag rolling gently to coat and cover. Refrigerate 4 to 6 hours or overnight. To serve, drain shrimp of excess marinade, place on a bowl chilled with ice or place in smaller dishes for individual servings.

This is a very simple dish that I like making with fresh South Carolina shrimp. It really has a great coastal Carolina feel to it. I have used store bought shrimp and it has worked fine. The fresher the shrimp the better.

Beaufort Shrimp Festival
Beaufort • 1st Weekend in October

Shrimp Festival is the first weekend in October each year and includes a run and walk plus a huge, exciting celebration of the shrimping industry. Enjoy local recipes and tastings. Shop in the craft market by the bay and browse the unique shops and galleries in the downtown historic district. Free entertainment, contests, and plenty of shrimp make this annual event unforgettable. The festival is held in historic downtown Beaufort at the beautiful Waterfront Park.

843.525.6644 • www.beaufortshrimpfestival.com

Lowcountry Shrimp Bake

3 pounds shelled, deveined shrimp
½ cup chopped red bell pepper
½ cup chopped sweet onion
1 (4.5-ounce) can sliced mushrooms
1 cup chopped celery
¾ cup milk
1 (10¾-ounce) can cream of mushroom soup
1 cup mayonnaise
1 tablespoon Worcestershire sauce
1 cup cooked rice or noodles
Salt and pepper to taste

You can use shrimp, scallops, clam, crab or any type of seafood you enjoy for this recipe. It is just as good in fall as it is during the summer. It has great taste with simple ingredients. We have served it at simple dinner parties and sometimes even at football parties.

Preheat oven to 375°. Steam shrimp or sauté in a small amount of butter; set aside. Sauté bell pepper, onion and mushrooms. Stir in remaining ingredients to combine flavors and spoon into a 9x13-inch baking dish. You can add an extra layer of rice or noodles to the bottom of the dish, if desired. It is a great way to increase portions. Bake about 30 minutes or until heated through and bubbly. Top with baked onion bits or buttered crumbled Ritz crackers during the last few minutes of baking for a great topping, if desired.

Lauren Caldwell, University of South Carolina

Lowcountry Shrimp and Cheese Grits

1 cup quick grits, plus ingredients to
    prepare per package directions
1 (7-ounce) package cheese spread
½ teaspoon minced garlic
2 tablespoons butter
2 teaspoons olive oil
1½ pounds South Carolina shrimp,
    shelled and deveined, without tails
1 (14.5-ounce) can diced tomatoes
    and chilies, or diced tomatoes
Salt and pepper to taste

*Lowcountry Shrimp and Cheese Grits
is a favorite around South Carolina
football game tailgates. And you can find
it on menus everywhere. I'm the parent
of several South Carolina graduates and
whenever I visit, it always seems like this
recipe is part of the trip.*

Cook grits according to package directions. Remove from heat and stir in cheese and garlic until cheese is melted. Cover and keep warm. In a skillet over medium-high heat, melt butter with oil. Sauté shrimp until pink. Stir in tomatoes and continue to cook until heated. Season with salt and pepper. Serve shrimp mixture over grits in individual bowls, or in a casserole dish.

Gerald Tidwell, Proud Gamecock Father, Columbia

Lowcountry Shrimp Festival & Blessing of the Fleet

McClellanville • 1st Weekend in May

Since 1976, McClellanville has rolled out the welcome mat for visitors from near and far to enjoy the Lowcountry Shrimp Festival. You'll find plenty of local shrimp, as well as options for non-shrimp eaters to enjoy. Live music makes this festival fun for everyone. Browse the official merchandise tent, the craft vendor area with more than 45 local artisans, or the huge children's play area. Make sure you've got a view of the creek for the main event: the Blessing of the Fleet. Join local clergy as they offer their blessings on the local shrimping fleet for a safe and bountiful season.

843.887.3323 • www.lowcountryshrimpfestival.com

Shrimp PoBoy with Homemade Remoulade Sauce

Homemade Remoulade Sauce:

¼ cup creole mustard
1¼ cups mayonnaise
1 teaspoon pickle juice
1 teaspoon hot sauce
1 garlic clove, minced
1 tablespoon paprika
1 to 2 teaspoons Cajun seasoning

Combine ingredients in a small bowl and refrigerate 30 minutes or longer.

Shrimp:

Vegetable oil for frying
¾ cup flour
¾ cup cornmeal
1 tablespoon Cajun seasoning

1 teaspoon salt
2 eggs, beaten
1 pound medium shrimp, shelled, deveined and tails removed

Add vegetable oil to a large frying pan to about ¼-inch deep. Place over medium heat; oil is ready when a small amount of flour dropped into hot oil sizzles. While oil is heating, combine flour, cornmeal and seasonings in a large bowl. Working with a few at a time, dredge shrimp in beaten eggs, then in dry mixture. Fry until golden brown on both sides, about 2 minutes. Remove to paper towels to drain. Repeat until all shrimp are cooked.

To Dress PoBoy:

4 soft French sandwich rolls
Mayonnaise or tartar sauce
½ head leafy green lettuce

2 to 3 tomatoes, sliced
Homemade Remoulade Sauce

Slice bread lengthwise without cutting all the way through. Spread bottom with a thin layer of mayonnaise or tartar sauce. Top with lettuce and tomato. Holding sandwich at an angle with the cut-side up, add a generous amount of shrimp, then top with Homemade Remoulade Sauce. Lay sandwich flat to serve, pressing it down with your hand to compress. (If any shrimp fall out, stuff them back in or just go ahead and eat one!)

Seafood Étouffée

1 stick (½ cup) unsalted butter
3 to 4 tablespoons all-purpose flour
½ sweet onion, chopped fine
½ tablespoon minced garlic
2 green onions, chopped
½ cup chopped green bell pepper
½ cup chopped celery
Water, up to 3 cups
½ cup milk
¼ cup chopped parsley
1 small bay leaf
Salt and pepper to taste
Hot sauce to taste
1 pound shrimp, peeled and deveined (if frozen thaw and drain well)
Cooked rice

This étouffée recipe lends itself to all types of seafood and doubles easily.

In a skillet, melt butter; add flour, stirring to blend. Cook, stirring constantly, until flour turns golden brown. Add onion, garlic, green onions, bell pepper and celery. Add water to cover by 2 inches. Continue to cook until vegetables begin to soften. Stir in remaining ingredients, except shrimp and rice. Simmer on low for about 10 minutes. Add shrimp and cook until just done, about 5 minutes. Taste for additional seasonings to your own taste and then serve hot over cooked rice. You can adjust the thickness by adding milk to thin, or cornstarch or flour to thicken. If you add too much water the flavor may suffer.

C. Jacobs

Beaufort Stew

1 pound smoked sausage links, sliced
10 frozen small corn cobs
10 small red potatoes
1 (3-ounce) package dry seafood seasoning mix
1½ pounds unpeeled, large fresh shrimp
Salt to taste

Beaufort Stew is a traditional South Carolina dish. There are many variations, but they all seem to include sausage, corn, potatoes, and shrimp. Some people call this a Lowcountry Boil or Beaufort Stew.

Brown sausage in large stockpot. Add corn, potatoes and seafood seasoning; add water to cover by 2 inches. Cover and boil 10 minutes. When potatoes are tender, add shrimp and cook until pink, 3 to 5 minutes. Drain and serve hot with additional seasoning, if desired.

*Mike Hicks, manager,
and the hometown employees of Southeastern Salvage,
Columbia*

Kent Whitaker

Kassandra's "Kinda" Lowcountry Crawdads

1 large onion, chopped
2 tablespoons chopped garlic
1 tablespoon olive oil
Salt and black pepper to taste
Dash cayenne pepper
2 cups half-and-half
1 cup chicken stock
1½ cups quick 5-minute grits
1½ cups grated Parmesan cheese
2 (12-ounce) packs crawfish or 2 pounds cooked shrimp

This is a neat combination of Lowcountry shrimp and down-home Southern grits.... So, it's kinda Lowcountry and kinda not!! Sometimes I just make the grits by themselves, they're so good.

In a medium saucepan, sauté onion and garlic in olive oil over medium heat. Season with salt, black pepper and cayenne. Add half-and-half and chicken stock; bring to a boil. Add grits and stir like crazy for 5 minutes. Reduce heat; add Parmesan cheese and stir like crazy. Stir in crawfish or shrimp. Cook until heated through.

Note: To bake this dish, place in greased casserole dish and bake at 350° about 10 minutes.

Kassandra Britt DeFranco, Greenville

Lowcountry Shrimp Seasoning

4 teaspoons onion powder
2 tablespoons garlic powder
2 tablespoons paprika
1 tablespoon ground mustard
1 teaspoon dried thyme
½ teaspoon pepper
½ teaspoon celery seed

I sprinkle this seasoning mix over everything from shrimp and grits to ribs on the grill. My mom called it Lowcountry Shrimp Seasoning, so I still do. She never ate much salt and I never add it.

Combine all ingredients and place in a small jar with a shaker top. Use as seasoning for broiled fish, poultry, cooked vegetables, soup and stews, or place it on the table to be used individually.

Karen Burns, Charleston

Lowcountry Cajun Festival
Charleston • 1st Sunday in April

Bringing Louisiana to South Carolina, Lowcountry Cajun Festival is a full-day of Zydeco music, Cajun and creole foods, children's activities and all around ragin' entertainment! Spend the day at beautiful James Island County Park as you savor the tastes of authentic Cajun and creole fare prepared fresh by local chefs. Enjoy jambalaya, alligator, étouffée, andouille sausage, and of course, crawfish, crawfish, crawfish! Also enjoy Lowcountry favorites like seafood and Southern barbecue. And, crawfish connoisseurs are invited to take part in the annual crawfish eating contest.

843.795.4386 • www.ccprc.com/cajun

Carolina Hot Tartar Sauce

1½ cups mayonnaise
¼ cup finely chopped onion
1 tablespoon hot sauce
¼ cup pickle relish
1 tablespoon creole seasoning
1 tablespoon Dijon mustard
¼ tablespoon minced garlic
½ tablespoon horseradish
½ tablespoon lemon juice

This recipe combines the creamy texture and flavor of a regular tartar sauce with a bit of extra flavor and heat.

Combine ingredients in a bowl, cover and chill before serving.

Classic Carolina Tartar Sauce with Capers

1 tablespoon chopped capers
1 cup mayonnaise
⅓ cup sweet relish
1 tablespoon lemon juice

½ tablespoon parsley flakes
1 egg, boiled and crumbled (optional)

Combine all ingredients in a bowl. Cover and chill until seafood is ready.

Cookies & Candies

Cream Cheese
Brownies, page 200

Charleston-Style Pirouettes

4 large egg whites, room temperature
1 cup sugar
1 cup flour
½ cup butter, melted
½ teaspoon vanilla
¼ teaspoon almond extract

Preheat oven to 350°. Beat egg whites and sugar in bowl until foamy, 30 to 45 seconds. Add flour, butter, vanilla and almond extract. Mix until well blended with no lumps remaining. Drop by unsmoothed teaspoonfuls well apart, 4 to 6 cookies at a time, on baking sheet. Flatten each piece into a thin circle, as even as possible, with back of spoon. Bake 6 to 8 minutes or until edges are browned. Remove and cool 15 to 20 seconds on baking sheet. Working quickly, immediately loosen cookie edges, lift cookie slightly and loosely roll around a wooden spoon handle. Do not roll too tight. Quickly slide off handle and cool on wire rack. Expect to damage a cookie or two as you practice.

Cathedral of Saint John the Baptist, Charleston

Crispy Almond Cookies

½ cup unsalted butter, softened
1 cup firmly packed brown sugar
1 large egg
1 teaspoon vanilla
⅛ teaspoon almond extract
1 cup all-purpose flour
1 teaspoon baking powder
½ teaspoon salt
½ cup chopped blanched almonds

You can also use pecans, walnuts, cashews, etc., for this recipe but the almonds really give it a wonderful flavor.

Preheat oven to 400°. In a large bowl, combine butter and brown sugar; beat with electric mixer on high until fluffy. Add egg, vanilla and almond extract. Beat until well blended. In a separate bowl, mix flour, baking powder and salt. Add flour mixture to butter mixture and beat on low just until blended. Stir in almonds. The dough will be very sticky. Drop equal-sized portions of dough, about a teaspoonful, about 2 inches apart onto a baking sheet coated with nonstick cooking spray. Bake 5 to 6 minutes or until edges are light golden brown. Cool 1 minute. Remove cookies with a spatula to wire racks; cool completely.

Jack's Favorite Cry Babies

½ cup margarine, softened
½ cup sugar
½ cup dark molasses
1 teaspoon ginger
1 teaspoon cinnamon
2½ cups flour
½ cup water
1 teaspoon baking soda
1 egg, beaten
Chocolate chips

This version of Delaware Cry Babies, a soft and delicious ginger-cinnamon cookie, was given to me by Jack's aunt and mother and are his absolute favorite. Jack insists that the 3 chocolate chips be point-up and centered. Any occasion that requires a gift is the time to present these 3-inch cookies to Jack. He hides them and may share just a few. Father of five, Jack needed to hide anything he cherished from the kids' colored pencils and markers—calculator, tape measures, truck keys, and especially these cookies.

In a bowl, mix margarine, sugar, molasses, ginger, cinnamon and flour. In a saucepan, bring water to a boil and add baking soda. Remove from heat and pour into flour mixture; stir to combine. Stir in egg; mix well. Drop by large spoonfuls onto greased cookie sheet. Arrange 3 chocolate chips on center of each cookie. Bake at 350° for 12 to 15 minutes or until puffy and firm to the touch.

Mrs. Jack Graham

Charleston Lighthouse

The lighthouse on Sullivan's Island was designed by United States Coast Guard designer and architect Jack Graham. The distinct triangle design has made the lighthouse a very distinctive structure for lighthouse enthusiasts to see. The lighthouse was designed in the late 1950s by Graham as one of his last official tasks. It was built in 1962 and is constructed of steel with an aluminum alloy skin. Graham did not know the lighthouse had been completed until he saw a picture of it in a magazine in the early 1960s. The lighthouse was built to replace one due to erosion. The island has been home to lighthouses for decades including one that was used during the Civil War.

Southern Snicker Doodles

½ cup butter, softened
½ cup shortening
½ cup sugar, divided
1¼ cups firmly packed brown sugar
2 large eggs
2 teaspoons vanilla

3½ cups all-purpose flour
2 teaspoons cream of tartar
1 teaspoon baking soda
½ teaspoon salt
4 teaspoons cinnamon

Preheat oven to 400°. Lightly coat baking sheet with nonstick cooking spray. In a bowl, beat butter, shortening, ¼ cup sugar, brown sugar, eggs and vanilla with an electric mixer at medium speed until well blended. In a separate bowl, combine flour, cream of tartar, baking soda and salt. Beat flour mixture into butter mixture at low speed until combined. Shape dough into 1-inch balls. In a shallow plate or bowl, combine remaining ¼ cup sugar and cinnamon. Roll dough balls in sugar-cinnamon mixture. Place 2 inches apart on prepared baking sheet and bake 6 to 7 minutes, or until cookies are puffed and crackled on top and the edges are set. The centers will be soft.

Charleston Lighthouse, 1962

Courtesy of USCG

Fresh off the Tree Persimmon Cookies

Pulp of 2 ripe persimmons
1 teaspoon baking soda
½ cup shortening
1 cup sugar
½ teaspoon vanilla
1 egg
2 cups all-purpose flour
½ teaspoon salt
¼ teaspoon ground cloves
½ teaspoon nutmeg
1 teaspoon cinnamon

When my husband and I bought our first home in West Ashley (a suburb of Charleston) the first thing I noticed was the beautiful tree in the front yard. As the seasons changed and fall rolled around I saw these gorgeous orange-colored fruits and thought to myself..."SELF...what are those—and whatever they are, I certainly can't let them go to waste!" Come to find out it was an Japanese persimmon tree! Doesn't sound so "southern" but apparently these trees are pretty popular around these parts. I learned to make persimmon cookies, persimmon pudding and even persimmon margaritas!

Preheat oven to 350°. Stir together persimmon pulp and baking soda. In another bowl, beat shortening, sugar and vanilla until creamy. Beat in persimmon pulp and egg. Sift in flour, salt and spices. Drop by spoonfuls onto greased cookie sheet. Bake 12 to 15 minutes. Will be soft and moist and delicious and fill the house with aroma and flavors of fall.

Leslie Haywood, Charleston
Inventor and founder of Grill Charms • www.grillcharms.com

Easy Plantation Cookies

1 egg
¾ cup packed brown sugar
1¼ cups all-purpose flour
½ teaspoon baking soda
¼ teaspoon salt
¼ cup vegetable oil
2 teaspoons vanilla
1 cup chopped roasted peanuts

These plantation cookies are very easy to make and use simple ingredients. There are many other versions, but this one is easy and makes for a very tasty cookie that is perfect when served warm. Be sure to use all-purpose flour, not self-rising flour. You can substitute pecans, cashews or walnuts, or even mixed chopped nuts for the peanuts.

In a large mixing bowl, beat egg with a hand-held electric mixer; beat in brown sugar. In separate bowl, combine flour, baking soda and salt; mix well. Add flour mixture to egg mixture a little at a time, alternating additions with oil. Stir in vanilla and peanuts. Drop by teaspoonfuls onto greased baking sheet. Bake at 375° for 6 to 8 minutes. Makes 2 to 3 dozen cookies depending on size.

Kelly Brown, for her dad Bill and his wife Jean of Ninety Six

Botany Bay Plantation and Wildlife Management Area, Edisto Island

WerksMedia/istock/thinkstock

Great Grandma Benjamin's Sour Cream Cookies

2 sticks (1 cup) butter or margarine, softened
2½ cups sugar, divided
2 eggs
1 (8-ounce) carton sour cream
4 cups sifted flour
3 teaspoons baking powder
1½ teaspoons baking soda

My mom always made these for me and they are one of my favorites. The recipe goes back to my Great Grandma Benjamin, who passed it down. Hope you enjoy.

Preheated oven to 375°. Cream together butter, 2 cups sugar, eggs and sour cream. Add flour, baking powder and baking soda; mix well. The dough will be soft. Take a teaspoon of dough and roll it in remaining ½ cup sugar, then roll it into a ball and place it on a greased cookie sheet. Bake 7 to 10 minutes.

Robbie Gawrys, North Greenville University

Riverfront Park, North Charleston

Brooke Elizabeth Becker/istock/thinkstock

Great Grandma Marsden's Orange Cookies

1½ cups sugar
1 cup butter
4 cups sifted flour
1 cup buttermilk mixed with
    1 teaspoon baking soda
2 eggs
1 teaspoon vanilla
1 orange, juiced and zested
3 level teaspoons baking powder
½ teaspoon salt

This recipe is from my mother, handed down from my Great Grandma Marsden. It's one we grew up on and my mother still makes them for us.

In a bowl, mix ingredients together and beat well. Let stand about 15 minutes. Preheat the oven to 350°. Drop by teaspoonfuls on a cookie sheet. Bake about 10 minutes. Ice while still warm.

Icing:

1 orange, juiced and zested
Powdered sugar

Combine to preferred consistency.

Robbie Gawrys, North Greenville University
In honor of Great Grandma Marsden

Benne Wafers

¾ cup butter
1½ cups brown sugar
2 eggs, beaten
1½ cups flour

½ cup sesame (benne) seeds
1 teaspoon vanilla
¼ teaspoon baking powder

Cream butter and sugar together and mix with remaining ingredients in the order given. Drop by teaspoonfuls onto well-greased cookie sheet, far enough apart to allow spreading while baking. Bake in a 325° oven for 7 to 10 minutes.

South Carolina Department of Parks, Recreation & Tourism

Knock You Nakeds

1 stick (½ cup) butter
½ cup light cream
1 cup sugar
1¼ cups flour
¼ teaspoon baking powder
¼ teaspoon salt

6 ounces chocolate chips
¾ cup maraschino cherries,
    drained and chopped
1 cup slivered almonds
½ teaspoon almond extract

Melt butter with cream and sugar. Cook over low heat until sugar dissolves; set side to cool. Sift together flour, baking powder and salt; divide in half. To ½ flour mixture, add chocolate chips, cherries and almonds; mix. Add cooled butter mixture; mix well. Add remaining flour mixture and almond extract. Mix well. Drop by spoonfuls onto greased cookie sheet and bake 15 to 20 minutes at 325°. Makes about 5 dozen.

Benne Seed Cookies

¾ cup butter, softened
1½ cups brown sugar
1 egg
1 cup all-purpose flour
½ teaspoon baking powder
¼ teaspoon salt
1 teaspoon vanilla
¾ cup benne or sesame seeds, toasted

Benne or sesame seeds were brought from Africa to our South by slaves. As they hoed the cotton they dropped the seeds at each end of the rows, thus making a border of benne plants. Also, the seeds were scattered over doorsteps to bring good luck. The seeds were roasted and used extensively in desserts and candies.

Preheat oven to 325°. Cream butter and sugar. Beat in egg. Sift dry ingredients. Add to butter mixture along with vanilla; mix just until combined. Stir in benne seeds by hand. Drop batter by teaspoonfuls onto buttered cookie sheet leaving room for cookies to spread. Bake 12 to 15 minutes or until lightly browned. Makes about 4 dozen cookies.

Natallia Khlapushyna/istock/thinkstock

White Chocolate Chip Cookies

2 sticks (1 cup) butter, softened
1 cup sugar
1 cup firmly packed light brown sugar
2 large eggs
2 teaspoons vanilla

3 cups self-rising flour
1½ cups old-fashioned oats
1 (12-ounce) package (2 cups) white
   chocolate chips

Preheat oven to 350°. Using an electric mixer, beat butter at medium speed until creamy. Add both sugars and beat well. Add 1 egg and beat just until mixed; repeat with remaining egg, then vanilla. Add flour, ½ cup at a time, beating continuously to incorporate. Stir in oats and white chocolate chips by hand. Drop by tablespoonfuls onto greased baking sheets. Bake 12 minutes. Cool on baking sheets about 2 minutes, then remove to wire racks to cool completely.

Glenys Gustin/istock/thinkstock

Pumpkin Chocolate Chip Cookies

1 cup butter or margarine, softened
1 cup packed brown sugar
¾ cup sugar
1 egg
1 teaspoon vanilla
2 cups all-purpose flour

1 cup quick oats
1 teaspoon baking soda
1 teaspoon cinnamon
1 cup cooked pumpkin
1½ cups semi-sweet chocolate chips

In mixing bowl, cream butter and sugars. Beat in egg and vanilla. In a separate bowl, combine flour, oats, baking soda and cinnamon; stir into creamed mixture alternately with pumpkin. Fold in chocolate chips. Drop by tablespoonfuls onto greased baking sheets. Bake at 350° for 12 to 13 minutes or until lightly browned.

South Carolina Department of Agriculture

Derby Bars

2 sticks (1 cup) butter, melted
2 cups sugar
4 eggs
1 cup self-rising flour
2 tablespoons vanilla
6 ounces flaked coconut
1 (12-ounce) package chocolate chips
2 cups walnut pieces
6 ounces butterscotch morsels

These derby bars started as a derby pie, but it was just more convenient to make them into cookie bars. This is now one of my favorite snacks.

Mix ingredients in order given. Pour into 9x9-inch brownie pan and bake at 350° for 45 minutes.

Meg Tarbox, Georgetown

Cream Cheese Brownies

Brownies:

½ cup butter
2 ounces (2 squares) unsweetened
   baking chocolate

1 cup sugar
¾ cup all-purpose flour
2 eggs

Preheat oven to 350°. In a 2-quart saucepan, combine butter and chocolate. Cook over medium heat, stirring constantly, 4 to 6 minutes until melted. Stir in sugar, flour and eggs until well mixed. Spread into greased 9-inch square pan. Bake 25 to 30 minutes or until brownies begin to pull away from sides of pan. Cool completely.

Cream Cheese Topping:

2 cups powdered sugar
3 tablespoons sweet cream butter,
   softened
3 ounces cream cheese, softened
½ teaspoon peppermint extract

5 drops green food coloring
2 drops yellow food coloring
Chocolate sauce or melted candy
   chocolate for topping

In small mixer bowl, combine topping ingredients, except chocolate. Beat at medium speed 2 to 3 minutes until light and fluffy, scraping bowl often. Refrigerate until ready to serve. Before serving, spread over cooled Brownies. Heat chocolate sauce or melt chocolate and drizzle over topping.

Dirty Brownies

1 cup all-purpose flour
¾ cup cocoa powder
¼ teaspoon baking soda
½ teaspoon salt
6 tablespoons unsalted butter, cubed
8 ounces bittersweet chocolate, chopped
¾ cup white chocolate chips or milk
    chocolate chips or peanut butter chips
4 large eggs, room temperature
½ teaspoon vanilla
1 cup sugar
10 ounces Dirty Monk Belgian-Style Porter
¾ cup semi-sweet chocolate chips
¾ cup chopped walnuts, pecans or macadamia nuts (optional)
Powdered sugar (optional)

This recipe is pretty cool. It uses Dirty Monk Belgian-Style Porter as an ingredient. But you can substitute your own Belgian Porter if you wish. For the Dirty Monk we use Trappist yeast, which gives the beer a sweeter flavor and a slight dark fruit finish.

Preheat oven to 375°. Coat a 9x13-inch baking pan with nonstick spray. In a medium bowl, combine flour, cocoa powder, baking soda and salt. Melt butter, bittersweet chocolate and white chocolate chips in a double-boiler over low heat, stirring constantly until melted. Remove from heat. In a large bowl, beat eggs, vanilla and sugar on high speed until light and fluffy, about 3 minutes. Continue mixing on low speed as you slowly add melted chocolate mixture. Then add flour mixture. Gently blend in Dirty Monk Belgian-Style Porter, being sure not to overmix. Add semi-sweet chocolate chips and nuts to mixture and pour into baking pan. Bake 25 to 30 minutes on center rack, until a toothpick inserted in the center comes out almost clean. When brownies have cooled, dust with powdered sugar, if desired. For an added treat, serve with vanilla ice cream and hot fudge. Enjoy.

Christopher McElveen, Thomas Creek Brewery, Greenville

Caramel Cheesecake Bars

1½ cups crushed vanilla wafers
1 cup chopped pecans, divided
¼ cup butter, melted (not margarine)
4 (8-ounce) packages cream cheese,
    softened
1 cup sugar
1 cup sour cream (not low-fat)
3 tablespoons flour
1 tablespoon vanilla
4 eggs
¼ cup caramel topping

Coat a 9x13-inch baking pan with nonstick cooking spray. In medium bowl, combine wafer crumbs, ½ cup pecans and ¼ cup melted butter. Press firmly into bottom of prepared pan; refrigerate until needed.

Preheat oven to 325°. In a large bowl, beat cream cheese and sugar with electric mixer on medium speed until well blended. Add sour cream, flour and vanilla; mix well. Add eggs, 1 at a time, while mixing on low speed. Pour over crust. Bake 45 minutes or until center is set. Refrigerate at least 3 to 4 hours.

Drizzle with caramel topping and remaining ½ cup pecans. Slice into bars and serve.

Valinda Davidson Wright & Family

Homemade Fig Bars

Filling:

1 cup sugar
8 ounces dried or fresh figs, finely chopped
½ cup finely chopped nuts (optional)
½ cup water if using dried figs (omit if using fresh figs)

According to the Clemson University Extension office, figs can be grown in most parts of South Carolina except for some mountain regions. There are about seven varieties. Why not make your own snack using fresh figs? You can also try this variation: Instead of making fig bars try using mini muffin cups. Use muffin liners, no cutting and perfectly sized individual bite-sized portions.

Combine sugar, chopped figs, nuts and water in a medium saucepan. Heat to boiling; reduce heat and simmer 10 minutes or until thickened, stirring frequently. Set aside to cool.

Crumb Crust and Topping:

1 cup brown sugar
½ cup margarine or butter
½ teaspoon salt

½ teaspoon vanilla
1¾ cups rolled oats
2¼ cups all-purpose flour, divided

Cream together sugar and margarine until light and fluffy. Add salt and vanilla; mix until blended. Stir in oats and 1¾ cups flour until well mixed and crumbly. Spread and pat ⅔ Crumb Crust mixture evenly into ungreased 9x13-inch pan.

Spread Filling evenly on top of crust. For Topping, add remaining ½ cup flour to remaining ⅓ Crumb Crust mixture; crumble and sprinkle over all. Bake at 350° for 25 to 30 minutes, or until lightly brown. Allow to cool in pan; cut into bars to serve. Makes 30 bars.

South Carolina Department of Agriculture

Lemon Shortbread Cookie Bars

¼ cup sugar
¾ cup powdered sugar
1 cup butter or margarine, softened
2 tablespoons grated lemon peel
¼ cup lemon juice
2¼ cups all-purpose flour
⅓ cup cornstarch
¼ teaspoon salt

Preheat oven to 325°. Grease bottom and sides of 9x13-inch baking pan with shortening, oil or nonstick cooking spray. In large bowl, beat sugar, powdered sugar and butter with electric mixer on low speed until combined. Then beat on medium speed until light and fluffy. Stir in lemon peel and lemon juice. Stir in flour, cornstarch and salt. Press dough into bottom of greased pan with floured fingers. Bake 35 to 45 minutes or until top is light golden brown. Cool completely, about an hour.

Lemon Icing:

2 cups powdered sugar
2 teaspoons light corn syrup
1 teaspoon grated lemon peel
3 to 4 tablespoons lemon juice

After bars have cooled, in a medium bowl, mix icing ingredients until smooth and spreadable, similar to butter. Spread over cooled bars and let stand until set. Slice and serve.

South Carolina Chocolate Pecan Pie Cookie Squares

2 cups all-purpose flour
1 cup dark brown sugar, divided
1 cup butter or margarine, melted
1 large egg, beaten
1 (14-ounce) can sweetened condensed milk
1 teaspoon vanilla
1 cup chopped pecans
Chocolate icing or topping of your choice

This recipe screams for a chocolate topping. The great thing is, you can use your favorite type—chocolate icing, candy-style hard chocolate topping, shaved chocolate, chocolate whipped cream, chocolate sauce drizzle; you get the picture.

Heat oven to 350°. Coat bottom of 9x13-inch baking pan with nonstick cooking spray. In a large bowl, combine flour, ½ cup brown sugar and melted butter. Spread over bottom of prepared pan. Bake 20 minutes. In a medium bowl, beat together egg, sweetened condensed milk, vanilla and remaining ½ cup brown sugar. Stir in pecans. Pour on top of baked cookie layer. Bake 25 minutes, remove from oven and allow to cool. When cooled, top with chocolate icing and cut into bars.

Downtown Columbia

SeanPavonePhoto/istock/thinkstock

Southern-Style Praline Squares

2 cups all-purpose flour
2 teaspoons baking powder
½ teaspoon salt
2 cups firmly packed brown sugar
2 sticks (1 cup) butter, softened

2 large eggs
1 teaspoon vanilla
1 cup chopped pecans
36 pecan halves
¼ cup powdered sugar

Preheat oven to 350°. Evenly coat a 9x13-inch baking pan with nonstick cooking spray. Combine flour, baking powder and salt in small bowl and set aside. Beat brown sugar and butter in medium bowl with electric mixer. Beat in eggs and vanilla until light and fluffy. Blend in flour mixture. Stir in chopped pecans. Spread batter in prepared pan. Arrange pecan halves on top. Bake 35 to 40 minutes or until center is set. Cool completely in pan on wire rack. Sprinkle with powdered sugar, then cut into equal portions. If you prefer, sprinkle with powdered sugar after cutting.

Carolina Beach Balls

1 package cheap lemon cookies
    (cream-filled or plain), crushed
1 (8-ounce) package cream cheese, softened
Shredded coconut to taste
4 (1-ounce) white or milk chocolate
    baking squares (or almond bark), melted

We make these when we visit the beach with the kids and need something to do when the rain comes or when we all just need a break from the sun.

Combine crushed cookies, cream cheese and coconut. Form into small balls. Dip each ball into melted chocolate (the kind that gets hard when it cools down). Place coated Beach Balls onto wax paper-lined cookie sheet; chill until chocolate hardens.

Lauren Caldwell, University of South Carolina

Carolina Coast Cherry Rum Balls

2 cups finely crushed vanilla wafers
1¼ cups powdered sugar, divided
½ cup finely chopped maraschino
   cherries

1 cup finely chopped pecans
¼ cup dark rum
3 tablespoons dark corn syrup
2 tablespoons unsalted butter, melted

In medium bowl, combine wafer crumbs, 1 cup powdered sugar, cherries and pecans; toss until well coated. Add rum, corn syrup and melted butter; mix very well. Chill 5 minutes and shape into ¾- to 1-inch balls. Roll balls in remaining ¼ cup powdered sugar until evenly coated. Place in container and cover tightly with lid or cling wrap, using toothpicks to keep wrap off balls. Chill over night. Yields 3 dozen balls.

Kelly Brown
for her dad Bill and his wife Jean of Ninety Six

Ivan MajrA1n/istock/thinkstock

Rena's Sugared Pecans

2 tablespoons butter
½ cup sugar

2½ cups whole pecans
1 teaspoon vanilla

Line a cookie sheet with parchment paper, or coat with nonstick cooking spray. I prefer parchment paper so the pecans dry evenly. Don't use wax paper. It just does not work well.

In a skillet over medium-high heat, allow butter to melt and sugar to dissolve. Add pecans and stir constantly with a wooden spoon to thoroughly coat. Remove from heat and stir in vanilla. Stir, stir, stir! Pour coated pecans onto prepared cookie sheet and spread apart as much as possible. Allow to cool completely. Store in airtight container.

Rena Keller, Sumter

Pecan Peanut Brittle

1 cup light corn syrup
1 cup sugar
1 tablespoon butter
¼ teaspoon kosher salt

2 to 3 cups roughly chopped pecans or peanuts, or a mixture
1 teaspoon baking soda

Slowly cook corn syrup, sugar, butter and salt in a nonstick pot over medium heat. Stir constantly until sugar dissolves. Don't scorch or it will become bitter. Add pecans and/or peanuts, and continue to stir until candy thermometer reads 290°. Remove from heat and quickly add baking soda. Stir like crazy for about a minute until mixed well. Before brittle starts to thicken, quickly pour out onto a greased cookie sheet spreading slightly as you go. I've used wax paper as well but prefer a greased cookie sheet. Don't over spread; it should be all the same thickness so it cools evenly.

Darnel Brantley, Clemson

Benne Sesame Seed Candy

2 cups sesame seeds
½ cup honey
½ cup packed light or dark brown sugar
½ teaspoon cinnamon
¼ teaspoon ground ginger

This candy is similar to making brittle.

Coat a 9x9-inch baking pan with nonstick cooking spray; set aside. Place sesame seeds into ungreased 10-inch skillet and toast over medium-high heat 5 to 10 minutes, or until lightly browned and aromatic. Combine honey, brown sugar, cinnamon and ginger in a large skillet. Bring to boil over medium-high heat, stirring constantly. As soon as mixture comes to rolling boil, cook exactly 2 minutes. Remove from heat and immediately stir in sesame seeds; mix well. Quickly, but carefully, spoon out hot mixture into greased pan. Dip a metal spatula into cold water and press candy into a very smooth and even layer. Cool candy in pan 15 minutes or until solid but still warm. Run spatula around edge to loosen. Turn out slab of candy onto wooden board or other cutting surface. Break in pieces or cut into small squares.

Charlotte Couchman/istock/thinkstock

Debra's Reindeer Crunch

5 cups Cheerios
5 cups corn Chex
2 cups peanuts (salted is best)
1 (21.3-ounce) bag holiday-colored M&M's
10 ounces mini pretzels
4 or 5 cups white chocolate chips
6 tablespoons oil

Debra Malone, my precious sister-in-law and fabulous lady of the kitchen here in Charleston, shared this recipe with me. I have made it for work parties and as a gift for my co-workers. I make enough to fill gift bags or boxes and it is a huge hit. Somebody has to say it—Thank you, whoever did it, for inventing corn Chex!!

In a large bowl, mix Cheerios, Chex, peanuts, M&M's and pretzels gently using your hands so pretzels won't break. Spread mixture out in a single layer on wax paper. Melt white chocolate chips with oil in microwave 3 to 5 minutes, stirring occasionally if needed. While chocolate is warm, drizzle over mixture on wax paper. Cool and break into pieces. It's fun to make and you can use any amounts of ingredients depending on your favorites. I have to admit, when my family makes this, we always add extra M&M's!

Dawn Malone Goldys, Charleston

Cakes

Cherry Sponge
Cake, page 223

Carolina Country Applesauce Spice Cake

2¼ cups all-purpose flour
1¾ cups sugar
1½ teaspoons baking soda
½ teaspoon baking powder
¼ teaspoon salt
¾ teaspoon cinnamon
½ teaspoon ground cloves

½ teaspoon ground allspice
½ cup butter, softened
½ cup buttermilk
1½ cups applesauce
2 eggs
¾ cup chopped walnuts

Sift flour, sugar, baking soda, baking powder, salt and spices into a large mixing bowl. Mix i n butter, buttermilk and applesauce. Beat 2 minutes with electric mixer on medium speed. Beat in eggs. Fold in chopped walnuts. Pour batter into a greased and floured 9x13-inch pan. Bake 50 minutes at 350°. Set aside to cool.

Pecan Cream Cheese Frosting:

¼ cup butter
1 cup chopped pecans
4 cups powdered sugar

1 (8-ounce) package cream cheese, softened
1½ teaspoons vanilla

Melt butter over medium heat; add chopped pecans. Stir constantly until browned; remove from heat and allow to cool. Mix powdered sugar, cream cheese and vanilla until smooth. Stir buttered pecans into cream cheese mixture. Spread Frosting over cooled cake.

Apple Streusel Cake

Streusel Topping:

¾ cup whole-wheat flour

½ cup packed brown sugar

½ teaspoon cinnamon

½ cup cold butter or margarine

In a small bowl, mix topping ingredients with pastry blender or fork until crumbly; set aside.

Cake:

1½ cups whole-wheat flour

1½ cups all-purpose flour

1½ cups sugar

3 teaspoons baking powder

1 teaspoon salt

1¼ cups milk

¾ cup butter or margarine, softened

1½ teaspoons vanilla

3 eggs

4 cups peeled and very thinly sliced apples

Preheat oven to 350°. Spray 9x13-inch pan with nonstick cooking spray. In a large bowl, beat all cake ingredients, except apples, with electric mixer on medium speed 3 minutes, scraping bowl frequently. Pour batter into prepared pan. Arrange apple slices evenly over batter. Sprinkle with Streusel Topping. Bake 55 to 60 minutes or until toothpick inserted in center comes out clean. Serve warm with ice cream or whipped cream.

Matthew Antonino/istock/thinkstock

Family Poppy Seed Cake

1 (18¼-ounce) box yellow or lemon
    cake mix
1 (3.4-ounce) box vanilla or lemon
    instant pudding
4 eggs
1 cup vegetable oil
1 cup cooking sherry or water
2¼ ounces poppy seeds

This is our family's favorite cake and has been shared many times with relatives and friends. It uses a box cake as a starter, which makes it very easy. It is delicious with both vanilla and lemon, making it hard to choose.

Preheat oven to 350°. In a large bowl, combine all ingredients and mix well. Pour batter into a well-greased Bundt pan. Bake 40 to 60 minutes.

Lynn Harper in honor of Mimi Flenniken and our South Carolina family, Darlington,

Jupiterimages/comstock/thinkstock

Rena's Sock-It-To-Me Cake

Filling:

2 tablespoons dry mix from 1 (18¼-ounce) yellow/golden cake mix
2 tablespoon brown sugar
2 teaspoons cinnamon
1 cup finely chopped pecans

Combine 2 tablespoons cake mix, brown sugar and cinnamon in medium bowl. Stir in pecans. Set aside.

Cake:

Remaining yellow/golden cake mix	**⅓ cup vegetable oil**
4 large eggs	**¼ cup water**
1 cup sour cream	**¼ cup sugar**

Preheat oven to 375°. Grease and flour a 10-inch tube pan. Combine remaining cake mix, eggs, sour cream, oil, water and sugar in a large bowl. Beat at medium speed with an electric mixer for about 4 minutes until smooth. Pour ⅔ batter into prepared tube pan. Sprinkle with Filling, then carefully spoon remaining ⅓ batter evenly over Filling. Bake about 50 minutes, or until a knife or toothpick inserted in center comes out clean. Allow to cool 20 to 30 minutes and remove from pan by inverting onto a plate or platter.

Frosting:

½ can vanilla frosting

When cake is cool, top with Frosting.

Rena Keller, Sumter, South Carolina

Qiana's Melt-in-your-Mouth Wet Cake

1 (18¼-ounce) box white cake mix, plus
   ingredients to prepare per package directions
1 cup milk
2 cups sugar
1 (16-ounce) carton whipped topping
1 (14-ounce) package shredded coconut

Growing up, we had desserts on special occasions only. My mother always cooked pies, but one year she introduced this special cake. I remember it like it was yesterday. I took one bite, and it was heavenly! Now, I am proud to say this has become my signature dessert. It literally makes people close their eyes and sigh. It is sweet enough to cure a sweet tooth, but not so sweet that you feel ultra guilty about having a piece before noon.

Prepare and bake cake in a 9x13-inch baking pan per instructions on package. When done, set aside to cool. For the "Magic Elixir", combine milk and sugar in saucepan. Bring to a boil over medium heat, stirring constantly. Cook 6 minutes, being careful not to scorch. Remove from heat and set aside.

When cake has cooled to lukewarm temperature, poke holes in entire surface with a toothpick. Quickly pour Magic Elixir over top of cake and let it soak in. Top with whipped topping and sprinkle with coconut. Refrigerate until serving time.

Note: To give your recipe a dose of local South Carolina flavor, purchase your eggs, milk and butter from Live Oak Farms in Woodruff, South Carolina. You can contact them at (864) 991-9839.

Soccer Player Qiana Martin, Seneca
www.qianamartin.com

South Carolina Coconut Cake

2 sticks (1 cup) unsalted butter, softened
2 cups sugar
2 teaspoons vanilla
4 eggs, room temperature

2⅔ cup cake flour
1 teaspoon baking powder
Pinch salt
1 cup milk, room temperature

Preheat oven to 350°. Butter 2 (8-inch) cake pans and line with parchment paper. In the bowl of an electric mixer, cream butter and sugar until light in color and fluffy, about 5 minutes. Add vanilla and beat until combined. Add eggs, 1 at a time, beating until incorporated.

In medium bowl, sift together flour, baking powder and salt. Add to egg mixture in 3 additions, alternating with milk, starting and ending with flour.

Pour batter into prepared pans and bake until top is golden brown and tester inserted into the center of cake comes out clean, 40 to 45 minutes.

Coconut Topping:

2 tablespoons water
1 teaspoon vanilla
2 tablespoons cornstarch
1¼ cups whipping cream

½ cup sugar
1 stick (½ cup) butter
2¼ cups sweetened flaked coconut
¼ cup sour cream

In a small bowl, stir water, vanilla and cornstarch until dissolved. In heavy medium saucepan, bring cream, sugar and butter to a boil over medium heat. Add cornstarch mixture and return to a boil. Remove from heat and stir in coconut. Cool completely. Mix in sour cream. Spread evenly over cake, cover and refrigerate overnight.

South Carolina Department of Parks, Recreation & Tourism

Chocolate Cake

1 (18¼-ounce) box chocolate cake mix
¾ cup chocolate milk
⅓ cup butter, melted
3 eggs
1 (8-ounce) container sour cream

1 (4-serving) package chocolate fudge
    instant pudding and pie filling mix
1 (12-ounce) bag semisweet chocolate
    chips (2 cups)

Heat oven to 350° (325° for dark or nonstick pan). Generously grease and lightly flour 12-cup fluted tube cake pan, or coat with baking spray with flour. In large bowl, combine dry cake mix, chocolate milk, butter, eggs, sour cream and dry pudding mix with spoon until well blended (batter will be very thick). Stir in chocolate chips; spoon into pan. Bake 55 to 65 minutes or until top springs back when touched lightly in center. Cool 10 minutes in pan. Turn pan upside down onto cooling rack or heat-proof serving plate; remove pan. Cool completely, about 2 hours.

Rich Chocolate Glaze:

¾ cup semisweet chocolate chips
3 tablespoons butter

3 tablespoons light corn syrup
1½ teaspoons water

In 1-quart saucepan, heat glaze ingredients over low heat, stirring frequently, until chocolate chips are melted and mixture is smooth. Drizzle over cooled cake. Store loosely covered until ready to serve.

South Carolina Campground Cook-Off
Calhoun Falls State Park • September

The South Carolina Campground Cook-Off was chosen as the winner of the coveted Bundy Award at the 2013 Governor's Conference on Tourism and Travel. The award is presented to an event that promotes rural tourism in the state. The cook-off is held at Calhoun Falls State Park, where the art of cooking over charcoal or wood creates an atmosphere of delightful aromas drifting from each campsite over Lake Richard B. Russell. Sponsored by Old 96 District Tourism Commission and Parks Division of the South Carolina Department of Parks, Recreation & Tourism, visitors are invited to come enjoy the beauty of nature and the best campfire cookin'.

1.866.354.0003 • www.sccampgroundcookoff.com

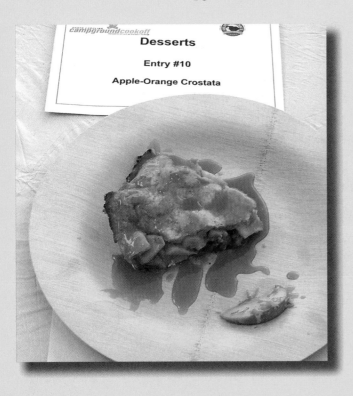

Camping Coke Cake

2 (21-ounce) cans cherry pie filling
1 (18¼-ounce) box chocolate cake mix
1 (12-ounce) can Coca Cola

Pour pie filling into a 12-inch Dutch oven. Cover evenly with dry cake mix and pour Coke on top. Do not stir. Bake over hot coals or on grill grate about 35 minutes or until cake is done.

Helen Morelli, Gilbert
South Carolina Department of Parks, Recreation & Tourism

Double Chocolate Zucchini Cake

2½ cups flour
½ cup cocoa
1 teaspoon baking soda
½ teaspoon salt
½ cup butter, softened
1½ cups sugar
½ cup vegetable oil

2 eggs, slightly beaten
1 teaspoon vanilla
½ cup milk
2 cups grated zucchini
6 ounces mini or regular chocolate
  chips

In a bowl, combine flour, cocoa, baking soda and salt; set aside. In a large bowl, cream butter and sugar; beat in oil, eggs and vanilla. Add milk, alternating with flour mixture until well blended. Gently stir in zucchini. Pour batter into greased 9x13-inch baking pan and sprinkle chocolate chips over top. Bake at 325° for 35 to 45 minutes.

Clemson University Extension Office

Harbour Town Marina, Hilton Head Island

Simple Chocolate Brownie Cake

½ cup cocoa
½ cup all-purpose flour
½ teaspoon baking powder
¼ cup canola oil
½ cup sugar

½ cup packed light brown sugar
½ cup egg whites (about 4 large),
  beaten until foamy
2 teaspoons vanilla
Powdered sugar for topping

Preheat oven to 350°. Grease 8-inch square pan. In small bowl, combine cocoa, flour and baking powder; set aside. In medium bowl, mix oil, sugar and brown sugar; stir in beaten egg whites and vanilla. Gradually stir in cocoa mixture until blended. Pour into prepared pan. Bake 15 to 20 minutes or until brownie begins to pull away from sides of pan. Cool completely in pan on wire rack. Just before serving, sprinkle with powdered sugar, if desired.

Slow Cooker Chocolate Pudding Cake

1 (18¼-ounce) box chocolate fudge cake mix, plus ingredients to prepare
  per package directions
1 (4-serving) package chocolate instant pudding mix
2 cups milk
2 (1-ounce) squares semi-sweet chocolate, coarsely chopped
  (or ⅓ cup semi-sweet mini chocolate chips)
2 cups whipped topping, thawed

Prepare cake batter as directed on package. In 3- to 4-quart slow cooker coated with cooking spray, beat pudding mix with milk until well blended. Pour cake batter carefully over pudding mixture, and cover with lid. Cook on low 2 to 3 hours or until toothpick comes out clean from center of cake. Top with chocolate; turn heat off. Let cake sit 30 minutes, covered, to allow pudding to set. When serving, be sure to dip down into cooker so you get some pudding with the cake, and serve topped with whipped topping.

Anne Cromis, Myrtle Beach

German Chocolate Candy Bar Cake

1 cup chopped pecans
1 cup shredded coconut
1 (18¼-ounce) box German chocolate cake mix, plus ingredients to prepare
   per package directions
15 bite-sized Almond Joy candy bars
1 stick (½ cup) butter, softened
1 (8-ounce) package cream cheese, softened
2 cups powdered sugar

Preheat oven to 350°. Grease a 9x13-inch glass baking dish with butter or nonstick cooking spray. Mix pecans and coconut and spread evenly on bottom of dish. Mix cake batter according to package directions. Chop candy bars into small pieces. (Candy bars may be chilled for easier chopping, but don't freeze.) Stir chopped candy bars into batter. Pour over coconut and nuts. Combine butter, cream cheese and sugar in a bowl. Drop butter mixture by tablespoonfuls on the batter. Don't spread. Bake 40 to 50 minutes.

Valinda Davidson Wright & Family

Cherry Sponge Cake

¾ pound fresh sweet cherries, divided
1½ cups all-purpose flour
1½ teaspoons baking powder
¼ teaspoon salt
2 large eggs

¾ cup sugar
1 teaspoon pure vanilla extract
¼ teaspoon pure almond extract
½ cup butter, melted and cooled
⅓ cup milk

Preheat oven to 400°. Treat a 3-quart glass baking dish with nonstick spray. Rinse, dry and pit cherries. Count out 14 cherries, cut in half, and set aside, cut-side down, on a paper towel (these will be for top of cake). Quarter remaining cherries and set aside. In a bowl, combine flour, baking powder and salt. Using an electric mixer, beat eggs and sugar about 3 minutes. Stir in extracts, cooled butter, and milk. Fold in flour mixture just until moistened. Gently fold in quartered cherries. Pour batter into prepared pan, smoothing the top. Bake 15 minutes then remove from oven. Quickly arrange cherry halves, cut side down, on top. Return to oven and bake 15 to 20 minutes or until golden brown and a toothpick inserted comes out clean. Place on a wire rack to cool. Serve warm or at room temperature.

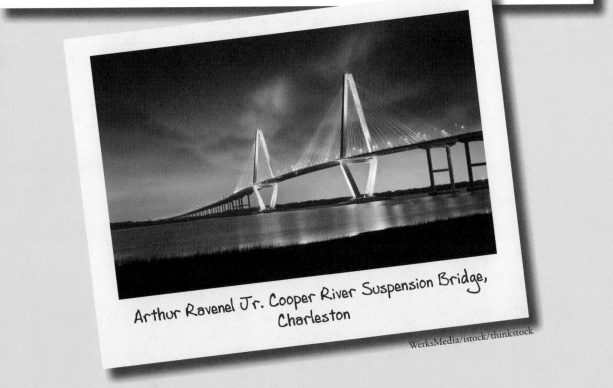

Arthur Ravenel Jr. Cooper River Suspension Bridge, Charleston

WerksMedia/istock/thinkstock

Lynn's Chocolate Chip Pound Cake

2 sticks (1 cup) butter, softened
3 cups all-purpose flour
2 cups sugar
1 teaspoon baking powder
½ teaspoon salt
¾ cup milk
4 eggs, room temperature
3 teaspoons vanilla
10 ounces (⅔ cup) semi-sweet chocolate mini chips

This cake recipe has been shared among our family and friends by actually writing down the ingredients, not from a cookbook! This is a real crowd pleaser.

Preheat oven to 325°. Cream butter. Add flour, sugar, baking powder, salt and milk; mix well. Add eggs, 1 at a time. Stir in vanilla and chocolate chips. Fold into well-greased Bundt pan. Bake at 325° for 1 hour and 10 minutes or until toothpick inserted near the middle comes out clean.

Lynn Harper in honor of Mimi Flenniken and our South Carolina family, Darlington

Easy Chocolate Chip Pound Cake

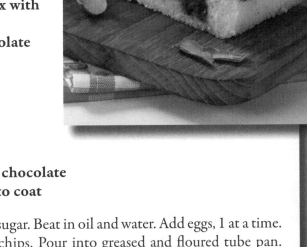

1 (18¼-ounce) box yellow cake mix with
   pudding
1 (1.4-ounce) box sugar-free chocolate
   instant pudding mix
½ cup sugar
¾ cup vegetable oil
¾ cup water
4 large eggs
1 (8-ounce) carton sour cream
½ (12-ounce) package semi-sweet chocolate
   chips, tossed with a little flour to coat

Combine cake mix, pudding mix and sugar. Beat in oil and water. Add eggs, 1 at a time. Stir in sour cream. Stir in chocolate chips. Pour into greased and floured tube pan. Bake at 350° for 60 minutes.

South Carolina Department of Agriculture

Blackberry Buttermilk Cake

A perfect cake for when you come home with a bunch of freshly-picked South Carolina blackberries.

1 cup fresh blackberries
2 cups all-purpose flour, divided
½ cup butter or margarine, softened
1 cup sugar
2 eggs
1 teaspoon baking soda
1 teaspoon cinnamon

1 teaspoon ground nutmeg
½ teaspoon salt
¼ teaspoon ground cloves
¼ teaspoon ground allspice
¾ cup buttermilk
Whipped topping
Chocolate shavings for garnish

Preheat oven to 350°. In a large bowl, gently coat blackberries with 2 tablespoons flour; set aside. In a mixing bowl, cream butter and sugar. Add eggs and beat well. Add baking soda, cinnamon, nutmeg, salt, cloves, allspice, buttermilk and remaining flour. Fold in blackberries. Pour batter into greased and floured 9-inch square baking pan. Bake 45 to 50 minutes or until cake tests done. Allow to cool; cut into squares. Serve topped with whipped topping and chocolate shavings.

Slater-Marietta Strawberry Festival
Slater • May

Join Foothills Family Resources to usher in summer at the Annual Strawberry Festival held on the grounds of historic Slater Hall. A benefit pancake breakfast begins the day, followed by a full day of family-friendly fun for kids, adults, and seniors. No entrance fee; tickets are purchased to buy food and crafts. Presented by North Greenville Hospital, the festival supports Foothills Family Resources and Blue Wall Group. These two community organizations nurture area citizens in stressful times, educate them on healthy diets, provide opportunities for further education and nourishment when cupboards are bare.

864.836.1100 • www.upstatestrawberryfestival.com

Very Strawberry Cake

1 (18¼-ounce) box white cake mix
1 (3-ounce) package strawberry
    gelatin mix
1 cup vegetable oil
½ cup milk

4 eggs
1 cup mashed strawberries
1 cup chopped pecans
1 cup flaked or shredded coconut

Preheat oven to 350°. Grease and flour 2 (10-inch) round cake pans. In a large bowl, combine cake mix with gelatin mix. Add oil and milk, beating at low speed. Add eggs separately, beating after each addition. Blend in strawberries, pecans and coconut. Pour batter into prepared pans and bake 30 minutes or until a toothpick inserted in the center comes out clean. Cool layers in pan on a wire rack for 10 minutes. Remove from pans, cool completely.

Strawberry Icing:

1 stick (½ cup) butter, softened
1 (16-ounce) box powdered sugar
½ cup mashed strawberries

½ cup finely chopped pecans
½ cup coconut

Cream butter and powdered sugar until fluffy. Add strawberries, pecans and coconut. Mix well. Frost cake with Strawberry Icing and garnish with fresh strawberries, if desired.

South Carolina Department of Agriculture

Barry's Favorite Orange Meringue Cake

Orange Filling:

2 cups and 2 ounces sugar
9 tablespoons flour
2 cups and 2 ounces orange juice
4½ tablespoons margarine, softened

In heavy saucepan, cook filling ingredients over medium heat, stirring constantly to keep from scorching, until very thick. Refrigerate.

Cake:

1 (18¼-ounce) box yellow cake mix, plus ingredients to prepare per package directions

When my husband, Barry, was a young boy, he found a picture of this cake in a magazine. He asked his mother, Mrs. Lottie Faye, to make it for his birthday, which she did. This has been his birthday cake ever since. I learned to make it when we were first married, and our daughter, Marie Wade Stephens, makes it also. Barry is now seventy-four years old, so it has been a long-cherished recipe.

Mrs. Wade (Granny) always had a habit of "sampling" her recipes before she would take them to church suppers. I once asked her why there was always a slice removed from whatever she was taking to a function. She told me that she "had to see if it was fit to eat!" From that time on, the church people, and others, KNEW which recipes were Mrs. Wade's and made a beeline to get whatever she had made.

Prepare and bake cake in 2 round cake pans per instructions on package, and cool.

Cut cooled cakes in half to make 4 layers. Place on a large round baking pan or jellyroll pan. Spoon cold Orange Filling between layers. Insert 4 large popsicle sticks through layers to bottom of cake to hold layers and filling in place. Refrigerate.

Meringue:

6 eggs, separated   **1½ cups sugar**

Preheat oven to 400°. Chill egg whites in a small mixer bowl along with the beaters and spatula. Beat chilled egg whites, adding sugar slowly, on high until stiff peaks form. Frost refrigerated cake with Meringue. Bake about 8 minutes to brown. Watch closely; do not burn. Cool then cover with plastic wrap (can use tall popsicle sticks to hold it off the cake). Refrigerate overnight before serving; refrigerate leftovers.

Janet Swope Wade, Aiken

Southern Living Taste of Charleston

Mount Pleasant • October

Southern Living Taste of Charleston is a three-day celebration of Lowcountry cuisine featuring favorite Charleston dining establishments. The kick-off event will showcase the best local chefs in a heated head-to-head battle in the Institute's state-of-the-art amphitheater kitchen. The Taste of the Arts on Gallery Row is where the talents of Lowcountry artists merge with the culinary arts. Guests will stroll through a dozen art galleries while sampling appetizers from a variety of Charleston restaurants. A celebration of Lowcountry cuisine is held at historic Boone hall Plantation and will feature Charleston's top restaurants offering samples of their signature dishes, as well as *Southern Living* editor appearances, editorial-inspired vignettes, demonstrations, giveaways and more.

843.577.4030
www.charlestonrestaurantassociation.com

Mandarin Orange Cake

1 (18¼-ounce) box golden butter cake mix (do not follow box instructions)
4 large eggs
1 (11-ounce) can Mandarin oranges (do not drain)
1 cup oil

Preheat oven to 325°. Mix all ingredients well. Pour into 3 greased, round cake pans. Bake until toothpick inserted in center comes out clean. Cool completely before icing.

Pineapple Icing:

1 (12-ounce) carton whipped topping
1 (3.9-ounce) box vanilla instant pudding mix
1 (15-ounce) can crushed pineapple (do not drain)

Mix together. Spread between layers, then spread an even layer of icing over top and sides.

Bobbie Coleman

Lady Baltimore Cake with South Carolina Peaches

1 (18¼-ounce) box deluxe white cake mix,
    plus ingredients to prepare per package
    directions (or make from scratch)
1½ cups sugar
2 teaspoon light corn syrup
⅔ cup water
2 egg whites
⅛ teaspoon salt
1 teaspoon vanilla
¼ cup raisins
¼ cup chopped figs
¼ cup chopped candied cherries
¼ cup chopped candied pineapple
¼ cup chopped pecans
1 to 2 South Carolina peaches, peeled, pitted and sliced

A Southern favorite—white cake with a luscious frosting and filling of figs, raisins, candied fruits, and pecans.

Using a cake mix or your favorite 2-layer white cake recipe, bake cake in 3 (8-inch) cake pans; set aside. Combine sugar, corn syrup and water in a saucepan; cook, stirring, over low heat until sugar is dissolved. Bring to a boil; when syrup mixture reaches about 234°, beat egg whites until stiff peaks form; add salt. Remove syrup mixture from heat when temperature reaches 240°, and immediately pour a very thin stream over stiffly beaten egg whites and salt, beating constantly. Add vanilla. Continue beating until frosting cools and is of spreading consistency, about 10 minutes. Add raisins, fruits and pecans to ⅓ of the frosting and use as filling between layers. Frost top and sides of cake with remaining ⅔ frosting. Just before serving, ring the bottom of the cake with South Carolina peach slices.

Peaches & Cream Cake

1 (18¼-ounce) box yellow cake mix
3 eggs
¼ cup oil

⅓ cup whipping cream
2 cups puréed peaches

Preheat oven to 350°. Coat bottoms of 2 (9-inch) cake pans with oil or nonstick cooking spray. Combine cake mix, eggs, oil and whipping cream. Mix until well blended. Add peaches; mix 1 additional minute. Pour into pans and bake 25 to 30 minutes. Cool completely on wire rack, and remove from pans.

Peach Frosting:

½ cup sugar
1 (3.9-ounce) box vanilla instant
   pudding mix

2 cups puréed peaches
1 (12-ounce) carton whipped topping

In a medium bowl, mix sugar, pudding mix and peaches. Stir well, then fold in whipped topping. Keep refrigerated. When cake has cooled completely, place 1 layer of cake on plate and frost; repeat with second layer. Refrigerate at least 1 hour.

2011 Peach Dessert Contest Winning Recipe by Estelle Willis

MarkVanDykePhotography/istock/thinkstock

Easy Red Velvet Pecan Cupcakes

1 (18¼-ounce) box red velvet cake mix, plus ingredients to prepare per package directions
1 (8-ounce) package cream cheese, softened
⅔ cup sugar
1 large egg
½ cup mini chocolate chips
½ cup flaked coconut
1 (16-ounce) tub cream cheese frosting
Chopped South Carolina pecans (optional)

Preheat oven to 350°. Grease muffin pans or line with paper baking cups. Prepare cake mix per directions on package. Spoon into prepared muffin cups to ½ full. In small bowl, combine cream cheese, sugar and egg; mix until smooth. Stir in chocolate chips and coconut. Spoon about 1 tablespoon cream cheese mixture onto middle of each muffin cup. Bake 25 minutes or until toothpick inserted in center comes out clean. Cool cupcakes. Spread frosting on top and sprinkle with chopped pecans, if desired.

Rebecca Brockie/istock/thinkstock

Nuttin' but Chocolate Beer Cupcakes

1½ cups all-purpose flour
½ teaspoon baking soda
2 teaspoons baking powder
¼ teaspoon salt
1 cup cocoa powder
1 cup chopped nuts (walnut, pecan, or macadamia)
3 tablespoons butter, softened
1½ cups sugar
2 large eggs
6 ounces Deep Water Dopplebock beer
1 teaspoon vanilla
1 cup milk

Sometimes you just need some chocolate cupcakes, and at Thomas Creek Beer, they are probably going to be beer cupcakes! Everyone says, "beer cupcakes?" And we all just giggle, because it sounds funny, but these are darned good cupcakes! This recipe uses our Deep Water Dopplebock beer from Thomas Creek Beer. DWD is a full-bodied German-style beer with a rich creamy flavor and South Carolina flare.

Preheat oven to 350°. Line muffin pan with paper liners, or prepare pan with a light layer of butter, oil or nonstick cooking spray and a dash flour. Sift together flour, baking soda, baking powder, salt and cocoa powder. Lightly cover nuts with a small amount of flour mixture to prevent them from falling to the bottom of the pan while cooking.

In a separate bowl, cream together butter and sugar until light and creamy. Add eggs, 1 at a time, making sure each is completely incorporated. When eggs are thoroughly incorporated add Dopplebock and vanilla. Add ½ flour mixture and beat thoroughly, followed by ½ milk. Repeat. Once batter is fully mixed, add nuts to batter and fold gently. Fill muffin cups ⅔ to ¾ full, as cupcakes will expand during cooking. Bake 18 to 20 minutes. Serve as-is or frosted with a topping of your choice.

Now, enjoy your treats with a cool glass of milk or the other half of the Deep Water Dopplebock (if you were able to refrain from finishing it during the baking).

Christopher McElveen,, Thomas Creek Brewery, Greenville

Peaches and Crème Cheesecake Cupcakes

Cheesecake:

3 (8-ounce) packages cream cheese, softened
5 eggs
1 cup sugar
1 teaspoon vanilla
1 teaspoon almond extract

Preheat oven to 300°. Combine Cheesecake ingredients in a mixing bowl; beat with electric mixer on medium speed until smooth. Place paper baking cups into muffin tins and fill cups ⅔ full with batter. Bake about 40 minutes.

These cupcakes are a real treat. If you bake often, you will not have a problem at all. If you don't bake, we suggest that you read over the recipe once or twice before baking, to plan ahead. We promise it is worth the extra few minutes! This recipe has three parts, all very easy, and wonderful when combined for the final tasty "peachy" finish. One note: use a spoon to push in the center of the cupcake in order to add a bit more of the cream filling. Think about it, who can be against more cream filling? Enjoy!

Sour Cream Filling:

1 cup sour cream
3 tablespoons sugar

1 teaspoon vanilla

Mix ingredients in a small mixing bowl using a spoon. When the cupcakes sink in the middle, place a scant tablespoon sour cream mixture in the middle of each one. Place back into the oven 5 more minutes. Remove from oven and cool.

Peach Mango Topping:

2 cups chopped fresh ripe peaches, divided
½ cup mango juice

⅓ cup sugar
2½ tablespoons cornstarch

Combine 1 cup chopped peaches, mango juice, sugar and cornstarch in a medium saucepan. Cook and stir over medium heat until mixture bubbles and thickens. Cool 10 minutes; add remaining 1 cup chopped peaches. Set aside.

When cupcakes are cool, spoon about 1½ to 2 tablespoons Peach Mango Topping on each cupcake and refrigerate.

South Carolina Peach Council

Sweet Potato Orange Kissed Cupcakes

2 cups sugar
2 sticks (1 cup) butter, softened
4 large eggs
1 (16-ounce) can mashed sweet
    potatoes
⅔ cup orange juice
1 teaspoon vanilla
3 cups all-purpose flour

1 teaspoon baking powder
½ teaspoon baking soda
1 teaspoon cinnamon
½ teaspoon ground nutmeg
¼ teaspoon salt
½ cup coarsely chopped pecans, or
    more to taste
1 (16-ounce) tub cream cheese frosting

Preheat oven to 350°. In a mixing bowl, cream sugar and butter using an electric mixer on medium speed. Add eggs, 1 at a time, beating after each addition until blended. Add mashed sweet potatoes, orange juice, and vanilla, beating on low speed. In separate bowl, combine flour, baking powder, baking soda, cinnamon, nutmeg and salt. Add flour mixture to sweet potato mixture a little at a time. Beat at low speed just until blended after each addition. Gently fold in pecans. Place baking cups in muffin pan; if using foil baking cups be sure to coat with nonstick cooking spray. Spoon batter into cups, filling only ⅔ full. Bake 28 to 30 minutes or until a wooden toothpick inserted into center comes out clean. Remove immediately from pans, and cool completely. Spread frosting evenly on top of cupcakes. Top with additional chopped pecans or chocolate chips, if desired.

The South Carolina State House, Columbia

SeanPavonePhoto/istock/thinkstock

Sweet Potato Cheesecake

We have to thank the South Carolina Department of Agriculture for this great recipe. Combining South Carolina sweet potatoes and a cheesecake—Genius.

Crust:

1½ cups graham cracker crumbs
¼ cup sugar
⅓ cup butter or margarine, melted

Combine graham cracker crumbs, sugar and butter in bowl. Press into bottom and 1 inch up the sides of 9-inch springform pan. Bake at 350° for 6 to 8 minutes. Do not allow to brown. Remove from oven and cool.

Filling:

3 (8-ounce) packages cream cheese, softened
1 cup sugar
¼ cup light brown sugar
1¾ cups mashed sweet potatoes

2 eggs
⅔ cup evaporated milk, undiluted
2 tablespoons cornstarch
¼ teaspoon cinnamon
⅛ teaspoon ground nutmeg

Beat cream cheese, sugar and brown sugar in large bowl. Beat in mashed sweet potatoes, eggs, and evaporated milk. Add cornstarch, cinnamon and nutmeg. Beat well. Pour into cooled Crust. Bake at 350° for 55 to 60 minutes or until edge is set.

Topping:

2 cups sour cream, room temperature
⅓ cup sugar

1 teaspoon vanilla

Combine sour cream, sugar and vanilla. Spread over warm cheesecake. Return to 350° oven and bake 5 minutes. Cool on wire rack. Chill several hours or overnight; remove side of pan to serve.

South Carolina Department of Agriculture

Pies & Other Desserts

Caramel Kissed
Apple Pie, page 250

Happy Cow
CREAMERY

The 1980's were devastating to the dairy industry and especially to this conventional dairy farm when milk prices were below the cost of production.

To survive as a dairy farmer, changes had to be made. The cows helped make the changes on this farm by breaking out of their confined area and into a field of lush April growth of lambs quarter, clover, and rye grass. The cows showed this dairy farmer a new way—"12 Aprils grazing." Planting forages year round proved to be an exceptional method of generating high-quality milk and reducing input costs drastically. This new method provided the opportunity to bottle milk on the farm.

The dairy farm is a 100-acre farm which serves no more than 90 Holsteins at a time. There are twenty-nine paddocks the cows rotate through, moving on 5,700 feet of "cow" roads. The grazing program provides year round "April" quality forages. The paddocks are planted with milk-making forages.

Happy Cow Creamery was built in October 2002, and is a unique facility in that the bottling plant is built in a Harvestore silo which had been out of operation as a silo for 16 years. This is the only Harvestore silo converted to a bottling plant in the world. It is an efficient unit bottling a gallon of milk every 4 seconds.

The on-farm store, which sells milk bottled right there on the farm, is also able to provide customers with local products grown in the area. Stone ground grits and cornmeal, pastured chicken and eggs, grass-fed beef, and artisan soaps (made from the milk) are only a few of the items for sale. The store also carries pure cream butter, and over 80 varieties of cheeses. Happy Cow Creamery partners with other local farmers to provide fresh, good food and milk that you will love!

Happy Cow Creamery

332 McKelvey Road
Pelzer, SC 29669
Store: 864-243-9699
Tours: hcctours@yahoo.com
www.happycowcreamery.com

From Grass to the Glass!

mksheldrake/istock/thinkstock

Granny Wade's Pecan Pie

½ cup sugar
1½ cups packed brown sugar
Pinch salt
2 tablespoons flour
2 to 3 eggs, lightly beaten
⅓ to ½ cup milk or cream
1¼ to 2 cups chopped or whole pecans
1 (10-inch) pie crust

Preheat oven to 350°. Combine sugar, brown sugar, salt, flour, eggs and milk; mix well, but don't overmix. Stir in pecans. Pour into unbaked pie crust; bake 30 to 40 minutes until pie is brown and set. Pie is done when all but a small circle in center is firm.

Marie Wade Stephens, Aiken

This recipe is always a big hit during the holidays for Christmas get-togethers. It has been used for generations in our family. My Granny Wade had many loving food stories in her 90 years of cooking. She was a retired South Carolina school teacher and a true southern Lady.

Pat's Pecan Pie

3 eggs
⅔ cup sugar
Pinch salt
1 cup dark corn syrup
⅓ cup butter, melted
1 cup pecan halves
1 (9-inch) pie crust

My family always serves this during the Thanksgiving holidays. South Carolina has some very good pecans across the state. This pie is very easy with simple ingredients. I hope you enjoy it.

Preheat oven to 350°. In a bowl, beat eggs thoroughly and stir in sugar and salt. Add corn syrup and butter. Mix in pecans. Pour into unbaked pastry shell. Bake about 50 minutes or until knife inserted in center comes out clean. Cool before serving.

Patricia Gullatte Britt, Greenville

Peaches and Cream Pie

2 pounds fresh peaches
1 (9-inch) pie crust, thawed
½ cup flour
½ cup light brown sugar
¼ teaspoon salt
1 stick (½ cup) butter, softened
½ cup sugar
½ teaspoon cinnamon
1 egg
2 tablespoons heavy cream
1 teaspoon vanilla

Wash, seed and peel peaches; slice thin and set aside in a bowl. If using a frozen pie crust make sure that it is completely thawed. In a bowl, mix together flour, brown sugar, and salt. Use a fork to blend in butter. Sprinkle ½ flour mixture evenly over bottom of pie crust. Place peaches on top of flour mixture. Sprinkle sugar and cinnamon over peaches. Whisk together egg, cream, and vanilla; pour over sliced peaches. Top with remaining flour mixture. Bake at 400° for about 45 minutes.

Country Peach Pie

½ cup sugar
¼ cup packed brown sugar
4½ cups sliced peaches
3 tablespoons cornstarch
¼ teaspoon ground nutmeg
¼ teaspoon cinnamon
⅛ teaspoon salt
2 teaspoons lemon juice
1 tablespoon butter
Pastry for 9-inch double-crust pie

Mix sugars in a large bowl; add peaches and toss gently. Cover and set aside for 1 hour. Drain peaches, reserving juice. In a small saucepan, combine cornstarch, nutmeg, cinnamon and salt; gradually stir in reserved juice. Bring to a boil over medium heat; cook and stir for 2 minutes or until thickened. Remove from the heat; stir in lemon juice and butter. Gently fold in drained peaches.

Line a 9-inch pie plate with bottom pastry; trim even with edge. Pour peach mixture into crust. Roll out remaining pastry. Cut into strips to cover pie with a lattice crust or cut decorative shapes to vent and cover pie with top crust. Trim, seal and flute edges. Cover edges loosely with foil. Bake at 400° for 50 to 60 minutes or until crust is golden brown and filling is bubbly. Remove foil. Cool on a wire rack before cutting. Delicious served as-is or topped with ice cream or whipped topping.

Cheesecake Pie

1 (8-ounce) package cream cheese, softened
½ cup plus 2 tablespoons sugar, divided
1 tablespoon lemon juice
1 teaspoon vanilla, divided
⅛ teaspoon salt
2 large eggs
1 (9-inch) graham cracker pie crust
1 cup sour cream
1 teaspoon cinnamon

This is one of my favorite recipes for Cheesecake Pie. It is pretty straightforward but I suggest you read over the directions because it is a two-part process.

In medium bowl, beat cream cheese until fluffy; slowly blend in ½ cup sugar. Add lemon juice, ½ teaspoon vanilla, and salt. Add eggs, 1 at a time, beating after each. Pour into graham cracker crust; smooth and bake at 325° for 20 to 30 minutes. When the center is set, remove from oven and allow to cool.

When cooled, combine sour cream, cinnamon, remaining 2 tablespoons sugar, and remaining ½ teaspoon vanilla; spread evenly over pie.

Rena Keller, Sumter

Elgin Catfish Stomp
Elgin • December

When the holiday season hits full swing, you know it's time for the parade season that kicks off the annual Elgin Catfish Stomp. Friday night gets everything started with the Catfish Stomp Pageant followed by the parade on Saturday. Elgin Catfish Stomp is a full 3-day schedule of parades, live entertainment, vendors, car show, and of course, mouth-watering catfish stew and fried catfish with all the fixings cooked by the Blaney Fire Department and volunteer firemen.

803.438.2362

Peanut Butter Pie

2 cups milk
4 eggs
½ cup creamy peanut butter
½ cup sugar
1½ teaspoons vanilla
1 (9-inch) pie crust, unbaked
Whipped topping (optional)
Peanut halves (optional)

Heat milk to warm; do not boil. In small mixing bowl, beat eggs with electric mixer on medium speed. Add peanut butter and continue beating. Mix in sugar and vanilla until well blended. At low speed, gradually beat in warm milk until smooth. Pour into pie crust. Bake on bottom rack of preheated 400° oven until knife inserted near center comes out clean, about 35 minutes. Cool on wire rack, then refrigerate. Garnish with whipped topping and peanut halves, if desired.

Fruit-Topped Buttermilk Pie

¼ cup all-purpose flour
1¾ cups sugar
½ teaspoon salt
8 tablespoons butter, softened
3 large eggs, lightly beaten

½ cup buttermilk
1½ teaspoons vanilla
1 (9-inch) pie crust, thawed if frozen
1 teaspoon ground nutmeg
2 cups fresh berries or sliced peaches

Preheat oven to 400°. Mix flour, sugar and salt in large bowl. Combine butter, eggs and buttermilk in a separate small bowl. Add to flour mixture and stir in vanilla. Spoon into pie crust. Sprinkle top with nutmeg. Bake 45 to 50 minutes on center rack. Cool on wire rack. Refrigerate until ready to serve. Serve with your choice of fruit on top.

Brookgreen Gardens,
just south of Murrells Inlet

RiverNorthPhotography/istock/thinkstock

Easy Lemon Chess Pie

1½ cups sugar
1 tablespoon Adluh flour
1 tablespoon cornmeal
4 eggs
½ cup lemon juice, or juice and
   rind of 1 lemon
½ cup melted butter
1 (9-inch) pie crust

Preheat oven to 350°. Combine sugar, flour and cornmeal. Add eggs, lemon juice and melted butter; mix well. Pour into unbaked pie crust. Bake 45 minutes at 350°.

South Carolina Department of Agriculture

Rena's Key Lime Pie

2 (14-ounce) cans sweetened
   condensed milk
1 cup key lime or regular lime juice
2 eggs
1 (9-inch) graham cracker pie crust
1 cup sour cream
2 tablespoons powdered sugar
1 tablespoon lime zest

Preheat the oven to 325°. In a bowl, combine condensed milk, lime juice and eggs. Whisk until well blended and pour into pie crust. Bake 15 minutes, then allow to chill in refrigerator at least 2 hours. In a bowl, combine sour cream and powdered sugar; spread on top of pie. Sprinkle lime zest on top and serve.

Rena Keller, Sumter

Darlington Pilot Club Sweet Potato Pies

2½ sticks margarine, softened
2¼ cups sugar
9 eggs, beaten
3 teaspoons vanilla
2 teaspoons cinnamon

1 teaspoon allspice
½ teaspoon salt
3½ cups cooked mashed sweet
   potatoes
3 (9-inch) pie crusts

Cream margarine with sugar, add beaten eggs, vanilla, cinnamon, allspice, salt and mashed sweet potatoes; mix well. Pour into 3 (9-inch) pie crusts; bake at 350° until crust is brown. Makes 3 pies.

Charleston Sweet Potato Pie

1 (9-inch) refrigerated pastry shell
4 tablespoons butter, softened
¼ teaspoon salt
1 cup sugar
3 tablespoons lemon juice
1 tablespoon grated orange rind
3 eggs, separated
½ teaspoon nutmeg
3 large sweet potatoes, cooked and mashed
1 cup light cream

Sweet potato pie is to the South what pumpkin pie is to New England.

Preheat oven to 425°. Line pie pan with pastry; flute edges. Cream butter, add salt and gradually beat in sugar until mixture is fluffy. Add lemon juice, orange rind, well-beaten egg yolks and nutmeg. Beat sweet potatoes with cream and add to butter mixture. Blend well. In small bowl, beat egg whites until stiff, but not dry; fold into mixture. Pour into pie pan. Bake 10 minutes. Lower heat to 350° and bake 40 to 45 minutes longer, or until a knife inserted in the center comes out clean. Makes 8 servings.

South Carolina Sweet Potato Festival
Darlington • 2nd Saturday in October

The South Carolina Sweet Potato Festival is a yearly day-long extravaganza held in Darlington, South Carolina, on the second Saturday in October. Held in the heart of downtown, birthplace of stock car racing, the festival fills the air with more than 25,000 visitors enjoying a variety of the 150 food/craft vendors, live entertainment, antique car show, door prizes throughout the day, and of course lots of sweet potatoes.

843.393.3526 • www.darlingtoncounty.org

Granny Wade's Sweet Potato Pie

3 large sweet potatoes, cooked, peeled and mashed
¼ cup flour
2 eggs, beaten
1½ teaspoons vanilla
1¼ cups sugar
½ cup milk
1 (10-inch) pie crust

Mix mashed sweet potatoes, flour, eggs, vanilla, sugar and milk. Put into pie crust. Brush the top with melted butter and sugar, if desired, to give the pie a crystalline look. Bake at 400° for 15 minutes. Reduce oven temperature to 350° and continue baking 35 minutes.

Janet Swope Wade, Aiken

This recipe is a great family recipe handed down through the generations. It's always a big hit, especially at Christmas and during the holidays.

Barry's Cherry Pie

Custard:

6 heaping tablespoons flour
2½ cups sugar
12 large eggs

½ gallon whole milk
1½ tablespoons vanilla

Combine flour and sugar in a large pot; mix well. Add eggs, milk and vanilla; stir constantly over medium-high heat about 30 minutes until thick. Watch closely, stirring in figure-eight motion to avoid scorching. Remove from heat and cool to room temperature.

Pie:

1 (2-count) Pillsbury refrigerated
    pie crusts
Sugar to taste

3 (15-ounce) cans sour cherries,
    drained well

Coat 2 (9x13-inch) baking pans with nonstick cooking spray. Spread 1 pie crust to fill bottom (not on sides) of each pan. Bake at 350° until brown; allow to cool. While crusts are cooking, combine sugar and cherries.

When Custard is cool, drain cherries a second time and add to custard. Spread over crust in 1 pan. Carefully remove crust from second pan (do not break), and place over cherries. Refrigerate if not eating immediately.

Janet Swope Wade, Aiken

Quick Blackberry Pie

1 cup plus 1 pint fresh blackberries, divided
½ cup sugar
¼ teaspoon salt
½ cup cold water, divided
1½ tablespoons cornstarch

1½ tablespoons lemon juice
3 ounces cream cheese, softened
3 tablespoons milk
1 (9-inch) graham cracker crust
Strawberry halves for garnish
Fresh mint for garnish

Wash blackberries thoroughly. Place washed berries on paper towels and pat gently to remove excess moisture. Place 1 cup blackberries, sugar, salt and ¼ cup water in medium saucepan. Bring to a boil and cook 3 minutes. Whisk cornstarch with remaining ¼ cup cold water; stir into saucepan. Cook, stirring constantly, until thick. Stir in lemon juice.

Beat cream cheese and milk together. Spread cream cheese mixture in bottom of graham cracker crust. Cover cream cheese mixture with half blackberry glaze. Arrange remaining 1 pint blackberries over glaze. Spoon remaining glaze over blackberries. Chill 2 hours. Just before serving, garnish with strawberry halves and mint.

South Carolina Department of Agriculture

millerv/istock/thinkstock

Caramel Kissed Apple Pie

2 (9-inch) pie crusts
½ cup finely chopped pecans
5 large Golden Delicious apples,
    peeled, cored and sliced
¾ cup packed brown sugar

2 tablespoons all-purpose flour
¼ teaspoon cinnamon
¼ cup butter, melted
Brown sugar to taste
Caramel sauce for topping

Preheat oven to 375°. Gently spread pecans across the bottom of 1 pie crust and gently press pecans into crust. Don't press too hard, you just want them to be secure enough to not move when the other ingredients are added. Toss apple slices with brown sugar, flour and cinnamon in large bowl. Carefully spoon apple slices into pecan-coated crust. You can either cut the second crust into strips and weave a lace pattern or keep the crust in one piece and simply cover the entire pie and cut a slit in the middle to vent. Drizzle melted butter over top crust. Bake on lowest oven rack for 1 hour or until crust is golden brown and apples are tender. Sprinkle the hot pie lightly with brown sugar and cool 1 hour. Before serving, drizzle caramel topping over crust. Serve with vanilla ice cream, if desired.

The Charleston Visitor Center Fountain,
Waterfront Park, Charleston

Devon Gustin/istock/thinkstock

Adluh's Sweet Potato Apple Cobbler with Pecans

30 ounces apple pie filling
1 pound Adluh Sweet Potato Mix
1½ cups whole milk
½ cup chopped pecans, plus more for topping
¾ cup light brown sugar
1 stick (½ cup) butter, melted

Adluh Sweet Potato Mix is a complete "table tested" mix that is easy to use. All you have to do is add water, milk or buttermilk. We make it in the tradition of our milling heritage which dates back to 1900. Traditionally in the South, sweet potato recipes tend to be for pies or baked casseroles with mini marshmallows which is fine. But we are a bit partial to this recipe. Of course, you could also whip up some sweet potato pancakes, waffles, and muffins by adding sugar, flavorings and spices.

Preheat oven to 400°. Pour apple pie filling into a 9x11-inch deep baking dish. Mix sweet potato mix, milk, pecans and brown sugar in a bowl. Pour over apple filling to completely cover. Sprinkle a few more chopped pecans on top. Bake 35 minutes until golden brown and completely cooked. Pour melted butter over top. Best when served warm.

Frank Workman, Columbia
Adluh Flour • www.adluh.com

Blackberry and Pecan Cobbler

2½ cups fresh South Carolina
    blackberries
1 cup sugar
½ cup chopped pecans
1 cup all-purpose flour

2 teaspoons baking powder
½ teaspoon salt
1 cup milk
½ cup butter, melted
Vanilla ice cream

In medium bowl, stir together blackberries, sugar and pecans; set aside. Preheat oven to 375°. Combine flour, baking powder, salt and milk. Stir in melted butter until blended. Spread batter in ungreased 8-inch square pan. Spoon blackberry mixture over batter and bake 45 to 55 minutes or until dough rises and is golden. Serve warm with a scoop of vanilla ice cream.

Rosemary Buffoni/istock/thinkstock

Butterscotch Peach Crisp

8 to 10 South Carolina peaches, peeled, pitted
   and sliced
¼ cup sugar
1 tablespoon lemon juice
¼ cup raisins
1 (3.9-ounce) butterscotch instant pudding mix
⅓ cup chopped dry roasted peanuts
½ cup flour
¼ cup rolled oats
½ cup cold butter

A Peach Crisp is a South Carolina dish worth sharing with the world! Whenever you can combine the taste of South Carolina peaches with butterscotch and bake it to a crispy treat—that's a good thing.

Mix together peaches, sugar and lemon juice in a bowl. Let stand at room temperature 15 minutes or until the peaches are juicy.

Preheat oven to 400°. Coat an 8-inch square baking dish with nonstick cooking spray. Place peach mixture and raisins in baking dish; set aside.

In small bowl combine pudding mix, peanuts, flour and oats; cut in butter until crumbly. Sprinkle over peaches and raisins. Bake 20 minutes or until bubbly around edges. Serve with ice cream.

South Carolina Peach Council

Rebecca Brockie/istock/thinkstock

Peach Crisp

3 cups sliced peaches or fruit of
    your choice
¾ cup flour
¾ cup brown sugar

¼ cup sugar
1 stick (½ cup) cold butter, cut
    into pieces

Spread peaches evenly in a 2-quart casserole dish. Combine remaining ingredients until crumbly, then sprinkle over top. Bake at 375° for 1 hour or until golden brown.

Quick and Easy Apple Crisp

6 cups peeled, cored and sliced
    cooking apples
½ cup unsifted all-purpose flour
½ cup quick oats

¾ cup packed brown sugar
1 teaspoon cinnamon
¼ cup butter or margarine

Place apple slices in 2-quart or 8x8-inch glass baking dish. Combine flour, oats, brown sugar and cinnamon in medium mixing bowl. Cut in butter until crumbly. Sprinkle over apples. Microwave on high 14 to 16 minutes or until apples are tender.

South Carolina Department of Agriculture

Apple Harvest Festival
York • 3rd Saturday in October

The apples are all picked and that means it is time to celebrate! Come out for the Apple Harvest Festival—a fall family tradition featuring all of Windy Hill Orchard's apple products plus hayrides, fresh picked apples, scarecrow making, apple cider tasting, live music, apple butter making, apple cider slush, pumpkins, carmel apples, blacksmith demonstrations, and much more. Drop by the Cider Garden to try our award winning Hard Ciders on tap!

803.684.0690 • www.windyhillorchard.com

Just Eat This
Two Apple Crumb

2 large Mutsu apples, cored and sliced
2 large Cameo apples, cored and sliced
12 tablespoons butter, divided
⅓ cup brown sugar
3 cups rolled oats
1 tablespoon cinnamon
1 teaspoon salt
2 cups chopped pecans

Preheat oven to 350°. Grease a 9x11-inch glass dish using 1 tablespoon butter. Combine brown sugar, oats, cinnamon, salt, pecans and remaining 11 tablespoons butter that has been cut into small pieces. Using your hands, mix until butter pieces are no larger than pecan pieces. Layer ½ apples in dish. Top with ½ oatmeal mixture. Finish layering with remaining apples and oatmeal mixture. Cover with foil and bake 30 minutes. Remove foil and continue baking 10 more minutes or until crumb topping is browned. For best results, allow to cool 30 minutes before serving.

Chef Chris Casner,
Just Eat This, Summerville

This is a great fall recipe. I was inspired to create this dish after talking with a local farmer at the market and discussing the different apple varieties. He suggested trying the Mutsu and Cameo varieties instead of Rome apples, and I was highly impressed by the taste.

South Carolina Strawberry Tart

2 tablespoons butter
2 cups miniature marshmallows
2½ cups rice cereal
1 (3.9-ounce) package vanilla instant
    pudding mix

1¼ cups milk
1 cup whipping cream
1 teaspoon almond extract
1 pint fresh strawberries

Melt butter in large saucepan over low heat. Add marshmallows and heat until marshmallows are melted, stirring frequently. Remove from heat and stir in rice cereal until well-mixed. Pat mixture into bottom and sides of an oiled 9-inch pie pan. (It may help to rub your hands with a little oil or butter.)

Beat pudding mix, milk, whipping cream and almond extract at high speed 5 minutes or until stiff peaks form. Spoon mixture into prepared cereal crust. Refrigerate at least 3 hours. Just before serving, wash strawberries and remove stems. Gently press strawberries stem-side-down into cream filling.

South Carolina Strawberry Festival
Fort Mill • 1st Weekend in May

The South Carolina Strawberry Festival is Fort Mill's signature salute to spring. Held each May in downtown Fort Mill, the Strawberry Festival offers five full days of family-friendly events and activities. Each year, the festival features hundreds of arts and crafts and vendors, three stages of live entertainment at the "Strawberry Jam," children's rides and activities, our popular "Berry the Competition" strawberry recipe contest, and of course, lots of delicious, locally grown strawberries! Other events during Strawberry Week include a golf tournament, gala, 5K walk/run, pageant, and strawberry picking at Fort Mill's Springs Farm. You won't want to miss the South Carolina Strawberry Festival. Come on out and join us.

803.547.2116 • www.scstrawberryfestival.com

Charleston Huguenot Torte

2 large eggs
1½ cups sugar
¼ cup all-purpose flour
3 teaspoons baking powder
¼ teaspoon salt

1 Granny Smith apple, chopped
 (about 1 cup)
1 cup chopped pecans
1 teaspoon vanilla
Whipped cream or ice cream

In a large bowl, beat eggs 5 minutes with electric mixer until they double in volume. Reduce mixer to medium speed and add sugar gradually; beat until tripled in volume. Gradually add flour, baking powder, salt, apple, pecans, and vanilla until well blended. Spoon batter into greased 9x13-inch metal baking pan. Preheat oven to 325° and bake 45 minutes or until golden. While baking, the torte will puff and then fall. When done, run a knife around edge of pan while still warm. Cut into 3-inch squares and top with whipped cream or ice cream.

Chocolate Nanner Pudding Trifle

Angel food cake
Vanilla instant pudding mix
Milk for pudding
Crumbled vanilla wafers
Sliced bananas
Chopped pecans
Whipped topping
Chocolate shavings or chips

Break up cake into small pieces and place desired amount of cake on bottom of trifle dish or individual bowls; set aside until pudding is ready. Prepare pudding in a bowl according to instructions on package. Layer prepared pudding and remaining ingredients over the angel food cake ending with whipped cream and a few sprinkles of chocolate chips. Serve as soon as possible after making.

This recipe uses no amounts because it's easy to swap out ingredients and use trifle bowls or even serving glasses.

Aiken Lobster Race
Aiken • 1st Friday in May

Conceived to spoof the Kentucky Derby and acknowledge the impact of the horse industry in Aiken, the inaugural Lobster Race was held in Aiken in 1984. Beginning as a small get-together of local friends, it has grown into a large festival and dubbed Aiken's biggest reunion. Former residents and visitors return to enjoy the Lobster Race and renew old friendships. Held the first Friday in May (day before Kentucky Derby) in downtown Aiken, the center of attention is the unique lobster track and band stage. Other attractions include children's rides, food vendors, and local bands completing the festival ambiance.

803.646.0523 • www.lobsterrace.com

Easy Berry Trifle

1½ cups cold milk
1 (3.9-ounce) package vanilla instant pudding mix
1 cup vanilla yogurt
6 ounces cream cheese, cubed
½ cup sour cream
2 teaspoons vanilla
1 (12-ounce) carton whipped topping, thawed (divided)
1 prepared angel food cake, cut into 18 (1-inch) cubes
1 pint blackberries, washed and drained well
1 pint raspberries, washed and drained well
1 pint blueberries, washed and drained well

You can use any available berries, or your favorites. You can also experiment with canned fruit but nothing beats fresh berries if you have them!

In a bowl, whisk milk and pudding mix for 2 minutes. Let stand 2 minutes or until soft-set. In a large bowl, beat yogurt, cream cheese, sour cream and vanilla until smooth. Fold in pudding and 1 cup whipped topping. Place ⅓ cake cubes in 4-quart trifle bowl. Top with ⅓ pudding mixture, ⅓ berries and ½ remaining whipped topping. Repeat layers once. Top with remaining cake, pudding and berries. Refrigerate until ready to serve. Trifles are best when served shortly after being prepared.

Death by Chocolate Trifle

1 devil's food cake mix, plus ingredients to prepare per package directions
2 (3.9 ounce) packages instant chocolate pudding mix, plus ingredients to
    prepare per package directions
1 (12-ounce) carton whipped topping
1 (12¼-ounce) jar caramel ice cream topping
1 (8-ounce) package English toffee bits or almond brickle chips

Prepare and bake cake according to package directions for an 8-inch square baking pan. Cool on a wire rack. Prepare pudding according to package directions.

Cut cake into 1½-inch cubes; place ½ in a 3-quart trifle bowl or large glass serving bowl. Lightly press down to fill in gaps. Top with ½ whipped topping, ½ pudding, ½ caramel topping and ½ toffee bits; repeat layers starting with cake. Cover and refrigerate until serving.

Peach Ice Cream

4 eggs, well beaten
1½ cups sugar
1 can evaporated milk
1 cup blended peaches
Whole milk to fill

Combine all ingredients and churn in ice cream maker until frozen. Mmm! Mmm! Good.

Fried Peaches and Ice Cream

Fresh or frozen peach slices
Honey
Butter
Brown sugar
Cinnamon

Drizzle peaches with honey. Melt butter in a hot skillet. Cook peaches in butter just to brown edges, sprinkle with brown sugar and cinnamon. Serve hot with ice cream.

Grilled Version:

Spread foil on counter top. Place peaches and butter on foil and drizzle honey over peaches. Sprinkle with brown sugar and cinnamon. Fold foil to seal and place the packet onto a hot grill. Grill about 10 minutes, turn and grill until done. Enjoy.

Actually, these can be enjoyed by themselves, but ice cream adds a wonderful creaminess. South Carolina is known for delicious peaches and this simple treat will please everyone. You can use frozen peaches, if desired, but fresh South Carolina peaches can't be beat for their exceptional flavor.

Lexington County Peach Festival
Gilbert • July 4th

Lexington County Peach Festival is a July 4 celebration of America at Gilbert Community Park with a variety of entertainment available throughout the day. Arts and crafts, children's rides, and a variety of foods, especially peach desserts and drinks, will be available for varying fees. The parade, entertainment on three stages, antique tractor & farm equipment display, car show, Revolutionary War re-enactment, volleyball tournament, and fireworks show are available at no charge. The parade begins at 9:30 a.m., and the fireworks show will begin at 10:00 p.m. Celebrated since 1959, the Gilbert Community Club sponsors the Festival.

803.892.5207
www.lexingtoncountypeachfestival.com

Pineapple and Pecan Guest Gelatin

1 (3-ounce) package cream cheese
1½ cups boiling water, divided
½ cup mayonnaise
1 (3-ounce) package flavored gelatin mix
1 (8-ounce) can crushed pineapple
½ cup chopped pecans

This recipe is delicious and light, and has been passed down as a family favorite.

Mix cream cheese and 1 cup boiling water in a large bowl. In a separate bowl, mix mayonnaise and remaining ½ cup boiling water. Combine cream cheese mixture and mayonnaise mixture well. Add gelatin mix, pineapple and pecans; mix well. Pour into a mold and chill until set. Stir occasionally during the first hour to prevent the nuts and pineapple from settling on the bottom. When the mixture starts to thicken there is no need to stir anymore.

Lynn Harper, in honor of Mimi Flenniken and our South Carolina family, Darlington

The Pineapple Fountain at Waterfront Park, Charleston

Judy Martin/istock/thinkstock

Brown Sugar Bread Pudding

Bread Pudding:

8 cups cubed French bread
5 tablespoons melted butter
4 cups whole milk
3 eggs, beaten
1 cup packed brown sugar

1 cup raisins
2 teaspoons cinnamon
2 teaspoons vanilla
Pinch salt

Put cubed bread in a 4-quart glass baking dish. In a medium bowl, combine remaining pudding ingredients. Pour over bread. Use a spoon to push all the bread under the liquid to completely soak. Set aside 45 minutes. Place dish in a cold oven, then set temperature to 350°. Bake, uncovered, 50 minutes or until set. Remove from oven to cool while making Caramel Sauce.

Caramel Sauce:

1 stick (½ cup) butter
1 cup packed brown sugar
½ cup evaporated milk

¼ teaspoon salt
1 teaspoon vanilla

In a small saucepan over medium-high heat, cook butter and brown sugar to bubbling. Add milk and stir well; bring to a boil. Boil 2 minutes and remove from heat. Stir in salt and vanilla. Pour over individual servings of warm Bread Pudding.

Charleston Lowcountry Bread Pudding

6 to 8 slices day-old bread
2 tablespoons butter, melted
½ cup raisins (optional)
4 eggs, well beaten
2 cups milk
¾ cup sugar
1 teaspoon cinnamon
1 teaspoon vanilla

Bread pudding is a Southern favorite as well as a Lowcountry and Gullah favorite. The recipes are endless as people used what they had on hand to make their bread pudding. We think you will enjoy this version. And, as with traditions, try some extra flavors of your own. If you don't have raisins, try pecans or dried cranberries!

Preheat oven to 350°. Break bread into small pieces and place in 8-inch square baking pan. Drizzle melted butter over bread. If desired, sprinkle with raisins. In a medium mixing bowl, combine eggs, milk, sugar, cinnamon and vanilla. Beat until well mixed. Pour over bread, and lightly push down with a fork until bread is covered and soaking up egg mixture. Bake 45 minutes, or until top springs back when lightly tapped.

South Carolina Festivals

The following is a list of annual festivals found throughout the Palmetto State. Chances are, we've neglected to include some events. If you aware of any we missed, call us toll-free 1.888.854.5954, and we'll do our best to include it in a subsequent printing. Keep in mind, too, that dates and venues change. Please verify all information before making plans to attend any of these events. Festivals are listed by month, then alphabetically by the city where the festival is held. Please call the number listed or visit the festival's website for more information.

JANUARY

Gaffney
Battle of Cowpens Anniversary Celebration
864.461.2828

Greenville
Greenville News Run Downtown • 864.444.4208

Mount Pleasant
Lowcountry Oyster Festival • 843.577.4030
www.charlestonrestaurantassociation.com

Orangeburg
Grand American Coon Hunt
Toll Free: 800.545.6153 or 803.534.6821

FEBRUARY

Beaufort
Beaufort International Film Festival • 843.522.3196
www.beaufortfilmfestival.com

Charleston
BB&T Charleston Wine & Food Festival • 843.727.9998
www.charlestonwineandfood.com • February-March

Low Country Blues Bash • www.bluesbash.com

Southeastern Wildlife Exposition • 843.723.1748

Lexington
Lexington's Race Against Hunger • 803.359.7770
www.lexrah.org

Port Royal
Bands, Brews & BBQ • 843.525.6257
www.fochospice.org

MARCH

Charleston
BB&T Charleston Wine & Food Festival • 843.727.9998
www.charlestonwineandfood.com
February-March

Charleston Festival of Houses and Gardens
843.723.1623 • March-April

Charleston International Antiques Show • Downtown
843.722.3405

Aiken
Aiken Spring Steeplechase • 803.648.9641
www.aikensteeplechase.com

Cheraw
Cheraw Spring Festival • 843.537.8420

Clover
St. Patrick's Day Festival • 803.222.9495

Columbia
Kids' Day Columbia • 803.545.3100

Palmetto Sportsmen's Classic • 803.734.4008

Easley
Easley Spring Fling • 864.430.9833
www.easleyfestivals.com

Florence
Big Brothers & Big Sisters BBQ Festival • 843.667.9512

Georgetown
Prince George Plantation Tour • 843.546.4358

Winyah Bay Heritage Festival • www.winyahbayfestival.org

Hartsville
Renofest Bluegrass Festival • 843.332.5151 or
843.332.1600 • www.renofest.com

MARCH (cont.)

Hilton Head Island
Hilton Head Island St. Patrick's Day Parade
843.384.4035 • www.stpatricksdayhhi.com

Hilton Head Wine and Food Festival • 800.523.3373

Shamrock Run • 843.757.8520

Wingfest • Shelter Park Cove • 843.681.7273
www.islandreccenter.org

Johns Island
Battle of Charleston • 843.559.0788
www.battleofchas.com

McConnells
Children's Day on the Farm • 803.684.2327

Moncks Corner
Shuckin' in the Park • 843.899.5200
www.oldsanteecanalpark.org

Myrtle Beach
Biker Bluegrass Festival • 843.369.5555
www.myrtlebeachharley.com

Canadian-American Days • 843.626.7444

Myrtle Beach Irishfest • 843.712.2618

Myrtle Beach St. Patrick's Day Celebration
843.997.6695 • www.mbdowntownstpats.com

Taste of the Coast • 843.272.8163

St. Helena Island
Penn Center Heritage Days Celebration • 843.838.2432

Summerville
Flowertown Run • 843.871.9622

Sumter
Morris College Fine Arts Festival • 803.934.3200
www.morris.edu

APRIL

Anderson County
Grand Anderson County Fair • 864.296.6601
www.thegreatandersoncountyfair.com • April-May

Belton
South Carolina Chili Cook-Off Championship
864.940.3111 • www.scchilicookoff.com

Blacksburg
Iron City Fest • 864.839.6006 or 864.839.1003

Camden
Camden Kitchen Tour • 803.425.7676

Cayce
South Carolina Tartan Fest • 336.499.9733
www.tartandaysouth.com

Central
Central Railroad Festival • Historic Downtown
864.654.1200

Charleston
Charleston Crafts Spring Artisan Market • 843.534.3036

Charleston Festival of Houses and Gardens
843.723.1623 • March-April

Earth Day Festival • 843.720.7111

East Coast Paddlesports & Outdoor Festival
843.795.4386

Lowcountry Cajun Festival • 843.795.4386
www.ccprc.com/cajun

Clarendon County
Clerendon Striped Bass Festival • 803.435.4405

Clinton
Living History Festival • 864.938.0100

Columbia
Columbia International Festival • 803.799.3452

Congaree Art Festival • 803.898.4921

Indie Grits Festival • 803.254.8234 • www.indiegrits.com

Pickin' & Piggin' in the Park • Saluda Shoals Park
803.772.1228 • www.icrc.net • April-May

South Carolina Cornbread Festival • 803.840.5270
www.sccornbreadfestival.com

Denmark
Denmark Dogwood Festival • 803.793.3734

Elloree
Pork Fest • 803.897.2821 • www.elloreesc.com

Florence
Arts International • 843.661.1225 • www.fmarion.edu

Pee Dee Plant & Flower Festival • 803.734.2200

Folly Beach
Folly Beach Sea & Sand Festival
www.follybeachfestivals.com

Fort Lawn
Fort Lawn Spring Festival • 803.872.4491

Greenville
Furman Earth Day Festival • 864.294.3655

Shalomfest • 864.292.1782 • www.shalomfestsc.org

Hardeeville
South Carolina-Georgia Border BBQ Cook-Off
843.784.3606 • www.hardeevillechamber.com

Hemingway
South Carolina BBQ-Shag Festival • 843.344.2527
www.scbbqshagfestival.org

Hilton Head Island
Art Market • 843.689.3033

Coastal Discovery Museum's Art Market • 843.689.6767

Hilton Head Island Seafood Fest • 843.681.7273
www.davidmcarmines.org

Indian Land
Indian Land Spring Festival • 803. 285.7416

Lamar
Egg Scramble Jamboree • www.lamareggscramble.com

Long Creek
Rholetter's Bluegrass Festival • 864.647.5768

Loris
Loris in Bloom Spring Festival • 843.756.6030

Mauldin
Hejaz Shriners Cook-Off • 864.505.8835

McCormick
McCormick Spring Bonanza • 864.852.2835
www.springbonanza.com

Meggett
April in Meggett Arts & Crafts Festival • 843.889.3622

Mount Pleasant
Lowcountry Strawberry Festival at Boone Hall
843.884.4371 • www.boonehallplantation.com

Town of Mount Pleasant Blessing of the Fleet & Seafood
Festival • 843.884.8517 • www.ComeOnOverMP.com

Myrtle Beach
Coastal Uncorked Food, Wine & Spirits Festival
843.626.9668 • www.coastaluncorked.com

Socastee Heritage Festival • 843.458.1461
www.socasteehf.com

Newberry
Pork in the Park in Newberry • 803.321.3685

North Augusta
Old Towne Artisans Fair • 803.279.7560
www.colonialtimes.us

Yellow Jesamine Festival • 803.441.4310

Pickens
Pickens Azalea Festival • 864.878.3258
www.pickensazaleafestival.org

Port Royal
Port Royal Soft Shell Crab Festival • 843.470.1110

Rock Hills
Come-See-Me Festival • 1.800.681.7635 or 803.329.7635
www.comeseeme.org

Springfield
Governor's Frog Jump • 803.258.3152

Summerville
Low Country Festa Italiana • 843.756.6030

Walterboro
Colleton County Rice Festival • 843.549.1079
www.ricefestival.org

West Columbia
Midland Plant and Flower Festival • 803.734.2200

Saint George
World Grits Festival • 843.563.7943
www.worldgritsfestival.com

Saint Stephen
Saint Stephen Catfish Festival • 843.567.3597

Spartanburg
Spartanburg Pow Wow • 813.765.03073

Summerville
Summerville Family YMCA Flowertown • 843.871.9622
www.flowertownfestival.org

Turbeville
Puddin' Swamp Festival • 843.659.2781
www.puddinswamp.com

MAY

Abbeville
Abbeville's Spring Festival • 864.459.1433
www.abbevillespringfestival.com

Aiken
Aiken Bluegrass Festival • 803.642.8966
www.aikenbluegrassfestival.org

Aiken Lobster Race • 803.646.0523 • www.lobsterace.com

Allendale
Allendale County Cooter Festival • 803.584.4619
www.cooterfest.com

Anderson
Blue Ridge Fest • 1.800.240.3400 • www.blueridge.coop

Anderson County
Grand Anderson County Fair • 864.296.6601
www.thegreatandersoncountyfair.com • April-May

Batesburg-Leesville
South Carolina Poultry Festival • 803.532.4601
www.scpoultryfestival.com

Beaufort
Gullah Family Festival • 843.525.0628
www.gullahfestival.org

Bluffton
Bluffton Village Festival • 843.815.2277
www.blufftonmayfest.moonfruit.com

Charleston
First Flush Festival • 843.559.0383, ext. 206

Charleston HarborFest • 843.722.1030, ext. 20

Cinco De Mayo Festival • 404.408.3657
www.charlestoncinco.com

Chester
Hog on the Hill BBQ Cook-Off Festival • 803.385.4803

State Capitol Building, Columbia

Henryk Sadura/istock/thinkstock

Columbia
BBQ Cook-Off & Festival • 803.782.1421, ext. 263

Pickin' & Piggin' in the Park • Saluda Shoals Park
803.772.1228 • www.icrc.net • April-May

Conway
Bluegrass on the Waccamaw • 843.222.2580
www.sccoast.net

Rivertown Music and Arts Festival • 843.248.2273

Fort Mill
St. Philip Neri Italian Festival • 803.548.7282
www.spnitalianfestival.org

South Carolina Strawberry Festival • 803.547.2116
www.scstrawberryfestival.com

Great Falls
Flopeye Fish Festival • 803.482.6029
www.flopeyefishfestival.com

Greenville
Artisphere • 864.271.9398 • www.artisphere.us

Enchanted Chalice Renaissance Faire • 864.271.4883
May-June

Greater Greenville Scottish Games & Highland Festival
www.greenvillegames.org

Piedmont Plant and Flower Festival • 803.734.2200

Greer
Greer Family Fest • 864.877.3131
www.greerfamilyfest.com

Hilton Head Island
Hilton Head Island Art Festival • 561.746.6615

Jamestown
Hell Hole Swamp Festival • 843.257.2430

Johnsonville
Johnsonville Heritage Festival • 843.386.3500
www.johnsonvilleheritagefestival.com

Johnston
Johnston Peach Blossom Festival • 803.275.2345
www.johnstondevelopmentcorp.org

Lancaster
Annual Red Rose Festival • 803.289.1498

Liberty
Spring Festival & Cruz-In • 864.506.0737

Little River
World Famous Blue Crab Festival • 803.795.9755
www.bluecrabfestival.org

McClellanville
Lowcountry Shrimp Festival • 843.884.4371
www.lowcountryshrimpfestival.com

Myrtle Beach
Beach Blast • 1.800.356.3016 • beachblastfest.com

North Charleston
Mayfest on Main • 843.280.5570

North Charleston Arts Festival • 843.554.5700

Orangeburg
Orangeburg Festival of Roses • 803.534.6821
or 1.800.545.6153 • www.festivalofroses.com

Pickens
YamJam: Papa John Foster Memorial Music Festival
864.878.4257

Rembert
Black Cowboy African American Cultural Festival
803.499.9663 • www.blackcowboyfest.tripod.com

Ridgeville
Edisto Indian Cultural Festival • 843.871.2126

Ridgeway
Art on the Ridge • 803.337.2213

Seneca
EFOC Memorial Weekend BBQ and Cook-Off
864.985.2841

Senecsa Fest • 864.882.9743, ext. 101

Simpsonville
Freedom Weekend Aloft • 864.228.0025
www.freedomweekend.org

Slater
Slater-Marietta Strawberry Festival • 864.836.1100
www.upstatestrawberryfestival.com

Spartanburg
Spartanburg Spring Fling • 864.596.2026

Sumter
Sumter Iris Festival • 1.800.688.4748 • www.irisfestival.org

Walhalla
Mayfest Art of Living • 864.638.2727

Ware Shoals
Ware Shoals Catfish Feastival • 864.554.7024
www.CatfishFeastival.com

Westminster
Mayberry comes to Westminister • 864.647.5316

Williamston
Pig in the Park • 864.934.4040 or 864.704.8131

Winnsboro
Wings and Wheels Air Festival • 803.635.4242

York
White Rose Arts Festival • 803.628.5132
www.whiteroseartfestivalyorksc.webs.com

JUNE

Canadys
Edisto Riverfest • 843.549.5445

Clover
Scotch-Irish Festival & Games • 803.222.9495
www.cloverscottishgames.com

Cowpens
Mighty Moo Festival • 864.463.3201
www.cowpensmightymoo.com

Greenville
Enchanted Chalice Renaissance Faire • 864.271.4883
May-June

Greenville Chautauqua Festival • 864.244.1499
www.greenvillechautauqua.org

Hampton
Hampton County Watermelon Festival
www.hcmelonfest.org

Mount Pleasant
Sweetgrass Cultural Arts Festival • 843.856.9732
www.sweetgrassfestival.org

Ridgeland
Taste of the Lowcountry Jasper Style
843.379.5430, ext. 233

Travelers Rest
The Swamp Rabbit Festival & BBQ Cook-Off
864.834.2388

Trenton
Ridge Peach Festival • 803.275.9487
www.ridgepeachfestival.com

JULY

Whitmire
Party in the Pines • 803.537.2535

Beaufort
Beaufort Water Festival • 843.524.0600
www.bftwaterfestival.com

Blackstock
Blackstock Fourth of July Festival • 803.519.9996

Gaffney
South Carolina Peach Festival • 864.489.5716
www.scpeachfestival.org

Gilbert
Lexington County Peach Festival • July 4th
803.892.5207 • www.lexingtoncountypeachfestival.com

Greenville
Red, White, and Blue Festival • 864.467.2776

Wing Ding 35 • www.wing-ding.org

Greenwood
Festival of Discovery • 864.942.8448
www.festivalofdiscovery.com

Pageland
Pageland Watermelon Festival • 843.672.6400
www.pagelandchamber.com

AUGUST

Darlington
Too Tough To Tame 200 NASCAR Camping World Truck
Series Race • 843.395.8499 or 866.459.7223

Jackson
Storks and Corks • 803.471.0291

Pelion
South Carolina Pelion Peanut Party • 803.606.9522 or
803.785.3272 • www.scpeanutparty.com

York
Summerfest in York • 803.684.2590

SEPTEMBER

Aiken
Aiken's Makin' • 803.649.1200 • www.aikensmakin.net

Aynor
Aynor Harvest Hoe-Down Festival • 843.358.1074
www.aynorharvesthoedown.org

Bowman
Annual Bowman Harvest Festival • 803.829.2666

Calhoun Falls State Park
South Carolina Campground Cook-Off • 1.866.354.0003
www.sccampgroundcookoff.com

Charleston
MoJa Arts Festival • 843.724.7305 • www.mojafestival.com
September-October

Columbia
Fall Festival • 864.656.3311 • www.clemson.edu
September-November

Columbia's Greek Festival • 803.461.0248
www.columbiasgreekfestival.com

Elloree
Trash to Treasures • 803.897.2821 • www.elloreesc.com

Fort Mill
ASC Greenway BBQ & Bluegrass • 803.548.7252
www.ascgreenway.org

Hardeeville
Hardeeville Catfish Festival • 843.784.3606
www.hardeevillecatfishfestival.org

Inman
Harvest Day Festival • 864.472.3654

Irmo
Irmo Okra Strut Festival • 803.661.1049
www.irmookrastrut.com

Murrells Inlet
Talaya Arts & Crafts Festival • 803.734.0450 or
843.237.4440

Myrtle Beach
Beach, Boogie and BBQ at Sun Fun Festival
803.493.2637 • www.smokeonthebeach.com

Nesmith
Williams Muscadine Festival • 843.355.7793

Newberry
South Carolina Elvis Festival • 888.406.5885
www.southcarolinaelvisfestival.com

North Myrtle Beach
Irish Italian International Festival • 843.281.2662

Simpsonville
Labor Day Fun Festival • 843.963.3781

Westminster
South Carolina Apple Festival • 864.647.7223
www.westminstersc.com

Winnsboro
Rock Around the Clock Festival • 803.635.4242

Yemassee
Yemassee Shrimp Festival • 843.589.2120
www.yemasseeshrimpfestival.com

OCTOBER
Abbeville
The Piedmont Blues and Hash Bash • 864.366.4600
www.bluesandhash.com

Anderson
Trojan Cook-Off • 864.231.2102

Beaufort
Beaufort Shrimp Festival • 843.525.6644
www.beaufortshrimpfestival.com

Bluffton
Historic Bluffton Arts & Seafood Festival • 843.757.BLUF
www.blufftonartsandseafoodfestival.com

Blythewood
Blythewood Balloons, Blues & BBQ • 803.754.0501

Cheraw
The South Carolina Jazz Festival • 843.537.8420
www.scjazzfestival.com

Columbia
Fall Festival • 864.656.3311 • www.clemson.edu
September-November

South Carolina State Fair • 803.799.3387
www.scstatefair.org

Conway
Live Oak Art & Music Fest • Downtown • 843.248.2273

Coward
Fall Frenzy • 843.389.2758

Darlington
South Carolina Sweet Potato Festival • 843.393.3526
www.darlingtoncounty.org

Fountain Inn
Aunt Het Festival • 864.862.2586
www.fountaininnchamber.org

Gaston
Collard and Barbecue Festival • 803.796.7725
www.gastonsc.org

Greenville
St. Francis Fall for Greenville • 864.467.2728
www.fallforgreenville.net

Jackson
Hook and Cook Festival • 803.471.2228 or 803.471.9778

Kershaw
Kershaw Hog Jam • 803.246.0369
www.KershawHogJam.com

Kingstree
Kingstree/Bi-Lo Pig Pickin' • 843.355.7484

Ladson
Coastal Carolina Fair • 843.572.3161
www.coastalcarolinafair.org • October-November

Laurens
Squealin' on the Square • 864.984.2119

Loris
Bog-Off Festival • 843.756.6030

McBee
McBee's Fall Festival At McLeod Farms • 843.335.8335
www.macspride.com

OCTOBER (cont.)

Mount Pleasant
Southern Living Taste of Charleston • 843.577.4030
www.charlestonrestaurantassociation.com

Myrtle Beach
Myrtle Beach Oktoberfest • 843.712.2618

Taste of the Town • 843.448.6062 • www.TOTMB.com

Newberry
Newberry Oktoberfest • 906.293.5562 or 1.800.831.7292

North Charleston
Latin American Festival • 843-795-4386
www.sc-charlestoncountyparks.civicplus.com

Olar
Model T's to Olar Festival • 803.368.5055

Orangeburg
Orangeburg County Fair • 803.534.0358
www.orangeburgcountyfair.org

Port Royal
Port Royal Festival of the Sea • 843.470.1110

Rock Hill
Old Town Blues & Jazz Festival • 803.329.8756

Spartanburg
Piedmont Interstate Fair • 864.582.7042
www.piedmontinterstatefair.com/

Travelers Rest
Trillium Arts Festival • 864.834.2388

Walhalla
Oktoberfest • 864.638.2727

Wellford
Mid-City BBQ Cook-Off • 864.463.4711

York
Apple Harvest Festival • 803.684.0690
www.windyhillorchard.com

NOVEMBER

Aiken
Blessing of the Hounds • 803.642.0528

Charleston
Charleston Holiday Market • 336.282.5550

Columbia
Jamil Shriners Craft Show • 803.772.9380
November-December

Greenville
Annual Greenville Holiday Fair • 864.233.2562
www.holidayfairgreenville.com

St. Francis Holiday Festival • 864.255.1040

Hilton Head Island
Hilton Head Island Oyster Festival • 843.681.7273
www.islandreccenter.org

Johns Island
Johns Island Harvest Fest • 843.795.4386

Mount Pleasant
East Cooper Crafter's Guild Craft Show • 843.566.1375
www.eastcoopercraftersguild.com

Myrtle Beach
Surfside Beach Turkey Trot Festival • 843.267.7443

Annual Dickens Christmas Show • 843.448.9483
www.dickenschristmasshow.com

Ridgeway
Pig on the Ridge BBQ Festival • www.pigontheridge.org

St. Helena Island
Penn Center Heritage Days Festival • 843.838.2432

Salley
Chitlin Strut • 803.258.3485 • www.chitlinstrut.com

Society Hill
Society Hill Catfish Festival • 843.378.4681

DECEMBER

Columbia
Jamil Shriners Craft Show • 803.772.9380
November-December

Elgin
Elgin Catfish Stomp • 803.438.2362

Myrtle Beach
Springmaid Beach Holiday Arts and Crafts Festival
866.764.8501 • www.springmaidbeach.com

Rock Hill
Christmasville • 803.329.8756
www.christmasvillerockhill.com

Index

Myrtle Beach

A

B

Hunting Island Light, Hunting Island

Jupiterimages/photos.com/thinkstock

RiverNorthPhotography/istock/thinkstock

Hometown Cookbook

Eat & Explore Cookbook Series

Arkansas
978-1-934817-09-4

Minnesota
978-1-934817-15-5

North Carolina
978-1-934817-18-6

Oklahoma
978-1-934817-11-7

Virginia
978-1-934817-12-4

Washington
978-1-934817-16-2

EACH: **$18.95 • 240 to 272 pages • 7x9 • paperbound**

Collect them all: EAT & EXPLORE STATE COOKBOOK SERIES is a favorite of local cooks, armchair travelers and cookbook collectors across the United States. Call us toll-free **1.888.854.5954** *to order additional copies or to join our Cookbook Club.*

State Back Road Restaurants Series

Alabama
978-1-934817-13-1
$18.95

Kentucky
978-1-934817-17-9
$18.95

From two-lane highways and interstates, to dirt roads and quaint downtowns, every road leads to delicious food when traveling across our United States. The brand-new State Back Road Restaurants Cookbook Series serves up a well-researched and charming guide to each state's best back road restaurants. No time to travel? No problem. Each restaurant shares with you their favorite recipes—sometimes their signature dish, sometimes a family favorite, but always delicious. This outstanding new series brings you terrific recipes plus a guide to those restaurants you won't want to miss while traveling the back roads. So crank up your car and join the fun.

EACH: **272 pages • 6x9 • paperbound • full-color**

Coming Soon...

Don't miss out on our upcoming titles—join our Cookbook Club so you'll be notified of each new addition.

www.GreatAmericanPublishers.com • www.facebook.com/GreatAmericanPublishers

State Hometown Cookbook Series
A Hometown Taste of America, One State at a Time

EACH: **$18.95 • 240 to 272 pages • 8x9 • paperbound**

The STATE HOMETOWN COOKBOOK SERIES captures each state's hometown charm by combining great-tasting local recipes from real hometown cooks with interesting stories and photos from festivals all over the state. As a souvenir, gift, or collector's item, this unique series is sure to take you back to your hometown... or take you on a journey to explore other hometowns across the country.

Georgia Hometown Cookbook • 978-1-934817-01-8

Louisiana Hometown Cookbook • 978-1-934817-07-0

Mississippi Hometown Cookbook • 978-1-934817-08-7

South Carolina Hometown Cookbook • 978-1-934817-10-0

Tennessee Hometown Cookbook • 978-0-9779053-2-4

Texas Hometown Cookbook • 978-1-934817-04-9

- Easy to follow recipes produce great-tasting dishes every time.
- Recipes use ingredients you probably already have in your pantry.
- Fun-to-read sidebars feature food-related festivals across the state.
- The perfect gift for anyone who loves to cook.

Order Form
MAIL TO: **Great American Publishers • P. O. Box 1305 • Kosciusko, MS 39090**

❑ **Check Enclosed**

Charge to: ❑ Visa ❑ MC ❑ AmEx ❑ Disc

Card# _____

Exp Date _____ **Signature** _____

Name _____

Address _____

City _____ State _____ Zip _____

Phone_____

Email_____

Qty.	Title	Total

Subtotal _____

Postage ($3 first book; $.50 each additional) _____

Total _____